COMMON SENSE SELLING

Van C. Deeb

To obtain further information, additional copies of this book, or to schedule Van as a speaker for your group, please write or call:

Van C. Deeb
12761 Izard St.
Omaha, NE 68154

In Nebraska: (402) 493-2430
In Arizona: (480) 659-5623

website: www.vandeeb.com
email: Van@vandeeb.com

978-0-615-29254-0

Printed in the United States by Morris Publishing
3212 East Highway 30
Kearney, NE 68847
1-800-650-7888

DEDICATION

I dedicate this book to all of you who want more, who spend the majority of your time trying to become better at your job.

I dedicate this book to those of you who stay up late at night dreaming about the way you would like to see your business grow.

I dedicate this book to those of you who close your eyes and visualize where you would like to see yourself next week...next month...next year...even years from now.

I dedicate this book to those of you who pray—not for money or material things, but for God to give you the ability to utilize your natural talents to not only fulfill your dreams, but those of others, too.

I dedicate this book to you.

This book will help you tap into your hidden strengths to accomplish your goals and dreams.

CONTENTS

● *From ground zero to a well-known Top Producer in Dallas, Texas* ● *Starting over in Omaha* ● *The birth of Van C. Deeb Realtors* ● *A company built by agents, for agents, to better serve our customers* ● *Community involvement, effective leadership pay off* ● *"People first" culture promotes steady growth*

● *What is sales?* ● *I believe. . .* ● *Build relationships* ● *Choose your words with care* ● *Dare to be different* ● *Strengths versus weaknesses*

"I challenge everyone reading this page to start saying hello today to everyone you make eye contact with and see how they react. It could possibly start a conversation or at the very least be the **bright spot** in someone's day. What I know for sure is the next time you see that person they will recognize you and you won't be a stranger anymore. This is a little thing we all can do that only requires a smile and a few words at best." Van C. Deeb

FOREWORD
by Tom Becka

I first met Van Deeb around 1993. He was a young, hard-working real estate salesman who was starting his own agency. To call it an agency is really a misnomer. It really was more of a dream than an agency. Van was a one-man shop working out of his garage.

He may not have had a secretary, or a lot of agents, or even a decent desk, but he had what he really needed. He had ambition, desire, belief in himself, tenacity, and heart.

Van truly loved selling real estate. He got personal satisfaction from helping a young couple buy their first home or helping a family relocate or expand into a bigger home.

With Van it wasn't about the commission and making more money (although he certainly made a lot). It was about the service. It was about trying to be better. It was about challenging himself and those around him to be better. To expand their boundaries.

And challenge himself he did. With each satisfied customer came a referral, and another, and another. I remember the excitement Van had when he finally moved into a "real" office—an office he didn't stay in long because his agency just kept growing and he had to move into a bigger space to handle all the business.

But while Van's business was expanding, so was his service to the community. Van has helped numerous children's charities and youth sports teams. And by helping these organizations he was helping himself by building goodwill. People remembered what a good guy he is when it came time to buy or sell a house. It was a win-win situation for all concerned.

Over the years I have learned a lot about sales from Van. I even use him as an example in my book *There's No Business Without the Show*—a book that combines many of the techniques I learned as a standup comic, salesman, and sales manager. You can buy it at amazon.com or a bookstore near you. (It might be wrong to promote myself when I should be writing about Van, but he's not shy about selling himself and neither am I. You've already bought his book; now go out and buy mine, too.)

Van recently sold his agency. That one-man shop grew to over 350 agents and hundreds of millions of dollars in annual sales. It's always inspirational to see someone live their dreams.

As I mentioned, I have learned a lot by having Van Deeb as my friend. I have learned by seeing how he operates—how he handles the ups and downs of business and life. I know that you, too, will learn a lot from reading this book. Enjoy!

INTRODUCTION

This book is designed to help you improve your sales skills. In addition to reading books and attending seminars, I've developed a set of common sense principles and techniques that have worked well for me. If you can implement just one of the ideas in this book, then your time will be well spent. I'm convinced that applying these techniques will increase both your sales skills and income.

I believe it's important to introduce myself as well as this book. That's why Chapter 1 describes how I got started in real estate and established a successful company.

Throughout my sales career, four main principles have guided my actions:

1. Sell from the heart.

2. Be assertive, sincere, and humble.

3. Treat every daily situation as a potential prospecting opportunity.

4. Set specific goals and through uncompromising focus, visualize reaching them.

These four principles are covered in Chapters 2 through 5, along with specific techniques that can help you become a more successful salesperson.

I'm confident that my success could not have been achieved without providing my customers with exceptional service. That's why Chapter 6 is devoted to this important topic. As a real estate agent, my goal was to treat each customer as if that person was at the top of my priority list.

People can tell when somebody is trying to *sell* them, and they don't like it. By personalizing your presentations, you can foster trust and a belief that you are the person who can best fulfill your customer's needs. This is the foundation on which all other aspects of the selling process are built, ensuring long-term business relationships and securing a referral base.

I believe in the power of quotations and affirmations, so I have provided some of my favorites in Chapter 7. I hope they will be as helpful to you as they have been to me.

You can feel confident that when you have practiced and internalized the common sense principles and techniques taught in this book, you will gain the results you have always wanted.

My career in sales has been both exciting and challenging. I hope you will feel the same way after reading this book.

The Story of DEEB Realty

For as long as I can remember, I've been intrigued by successful leaders and attracted to leadership roles. If I can't lead the crowd, I don't want to be part of the crowd. I knew that in sales, my results would reflect the amount of effort I put into my career instead of someone else's idea of what I was worth. That's why I decided to enter the real estate industry. As you'll see in this chapter, my chosen career has taken me down some exciting and unexpected paths. Throughout this book, I'll share a number of common sense philosophies and techniques that have helped me achieve my goals. By applying them to your own career, you can get results that will surprise you. Let the journey begin!

From Ground Zero to a Well-Known Top Producer in Dallas, Texas

I was involved in real estate for 12 years before starting my own company. My real estate career began at age 22 when I moved from Omaha, Nebraska, to Dallas, Texas. I moved to Dallas because I wanted to spread my wings and see what it was like to live in a different place. I was planning to go to real estate school at some point and then come back to Omaha and set the world on fire. Dallas was the number one real estate market in the country at that time, so I

> *Most people have greatness inside, but they never learn how to use it.*

decided to get my feet wet in the Dallas market. Real estate sales quickly became my passion, and I couldn't get enough of it. It was an addiction more powerful and exciting than anything I had ever experienced.

My goal was to be number one. I didn't want to just be a good agent; I wanted to be the best. I did some research and found out that the number one agent in the city was a lady at RE/MAX who had been doing it for more than 20 years. Everybody talked about her nonstop, so I decided to call and invite her to lunch. Even though I didn't know anything about real estate and I was a couple of years out of college, she agreed to have lunch with me. As I was talking with her, I realized that she wasn't so different from me. The main difference was that she was selling an incredible amount of real estate and I was just getting started.

I left that meeting so high that I couldn't even talk. I had never felt my adrenaline flow like that before, not even during a football game when I picked off a pass and scored a touchdown in the spring game in college. I left that meeting thinking, "I know I can be number one now. Nothing can stop me." Within three months I was number one in sales for a national home builder, and during my first year as a licensed agent I was Rookie of the Year for the state of Texas.

By age 30 I was listed in the top 1 percent of all agents in the United States, and my name had become a household word throughout Dallas.

Starting Over in Omaha

Sometimes life throws you a curve that ends up leading to bigger and better things. I became a father in 1988, and I decided to move back to Omaha a couple of years after my daughter Courtney was born. Even though Dallas was a great place to live, there were no family members in the area who could help me with my daughter, and she was my number one priority. I had always planned to return to Omaha at some point in my life, and I figured now was the time to do it. I told my staff I was moving, and it took me six months to thank past customers and friends before I completely finished my business there. They actually thought something was wrong with me because you don't build what I'd built and just walk away from it. But I knew I was making the right decision because that little girl of mine was my world.

I made the move and was glad I did, because it increased by tenfold the amount of time I was able to spend with my daughter. Courtney came to Omaha for holidays and for two to three months every summer, and not only was she able to spend time with me but also with her grandparents, uncles, aunts, and cousins. She eventually lived with me full time to attend high school in Omaha.

Back then CBS and Home were two separate real estate companies, and they each offered me relocation

> *Associate only with people who share or respect your positive attitude and desire for success.*

packages to move back to Omaha. That isn't a common practice in the real estate business, but they knew what I had accomplished in Dallas and what I could do for them. I had sent each company a book containing about a hundred newspaper articles about me, so they knew I wasn't just some Joe Schmoe coming back to Omaha to sell real estate.

Both companies made a really big deal about me, and of course when people make a big deal about somebody it creates a lot of jealousy. I decided to go with CBS, and they moved a long-time salesperson out of her office so I could have an office. As a result of all this attention some of the other agents prejudged me, thinking I saw myself as some kind of big shot—that I was arrogant and all the other things that jealous people assume.

At CBS I worked hard to establish myself and reconnect with friends and family. Within the first six months I was one of the top 15 producers in the company. I had worked day and night seven days a week to establish myself as a top Realtor in Omaha and build on the reputation I had established as an agent in Dallas.

The Birth of Van C. Deeb Realtors

Not long after I started working for CBS, it became clear that my philosophy about what represents a good environment for a real estate agent was different from theirs. Within seven months I had decided to start my own company. Please know that I have a tremendous amount of respect for CBS HOME Realty—we just had two different thought patterns.

One area of disagreement involved listings. I believe that when a real estate agent gets a listing and puts a sign in the front yard of a house, the listing agent should get the leads from the sign. Anybody calling because of that sign should be sent directly to the agent who listed the property. At that time, however, it was common for real estate firms to have what they called a "Duty Desk." Agents took turns sitting behind the receptionist, and if a prospective buyer called about a certain address the lead would be given to the agent who was on Duty Desk at the time. After working hard to get listings, I felt that the calls for my listings should go directly to me instead of some other agent who happened to be on Duty Desk at the time of the call. I knew the sellers and I knew the house inside and out, so I should be the one to get that call. Starting my own company meant I would get the leads from all my listings as an agent should, reflecting my common sense approach to doing business.

My second area of disagreement involved commission payments. In Omaha at that time, agents had to wait two to five days after a closing to get paid.

In Dallas, by contrast, an agent could count on receiving the commission check the same day as the closing. To me, it made more sense to pay the agents immediately, since they were the ones who kept the agency going.

Deciding to go out on my own was pretty easy. When you work for a real estate firm you're an independent contractor on straight commission, with no consistent paycheck coming in. After being an independent contractor for 12 years I knew I could make it on my own.

I took the Nebraska real estate broker's exam and waited for the results. Today you take the test and find out on the spot whether you passed or failed, but back in 1993 I had to check my mailbox daily for the letter saying whether I had passed the test. I'll never forget the day when I checked my mailbox and found a letter from the Nebraska Real Estate Commission that said, "Congratulations on passing your broker's exam." I remember standing outside my condo next to the mailbox, holding the letter up in the air and yelling, "Things are going to start happening now!" I got that line from a Steve Martin movie called "The Jerk" where the main character saw his name in the phone directory for the first time and said, "Things are going to start happening now." Although I wasn't the first person to make that statement, it fit the occasion perfectly.

When I started Van C. Deeb Realtors on December 9, 1993, I thought it was going to be a one-person operation that I would run from my house. I knew that working for a specific company did not guarantee success, and agents would be successful if they had enough drive, desire, and determination to succeed. With this in mind, I was confident that I was going to do okay.

I started out by hitting the streets hard, doing open houses and convincing people to use me as their agent. A big challenge during my first two years in business involved educating buyers and sellers that even though they'd never heard of Van C. Deeb Realtors and it was a brand new company, it was okay to use me because I was going to do everything that I would have done for them if I worked at a big firm. My ability, not the name of the agency, would help them sell or buy a house.

When I was getting ready to start my own company, two of the largest real estate firms in Omaha told me there was no room for another real estate company in the city and there was no sense in trying to start one because it wasn't going to work. They tried to convince me to go to their firm and be a manager ("Oh, boy!") or stay with their firm instead of starting my own. It turned out that they were wrong. Over the next 15 years my company grew from a one-person operation to more than 350 associates, becoming one of the largest independent real estate companies in the Midwest and the third largest in Omaha.

It was pretty cool building a company from scratch instead of inheriting it from family members as several competitors of mine had done. It sure taught me a lot about hard work—and praying a lot didn't hurt, either.

A Company Built by Agents, for Agents, to Better Serve Our Customers

Van C. Deeb Realtors started out pretty small. It was a one-person operation in the beginning, but then agents from the other real estate firms started saying, "I like the way you do business. Have you ever thought about bringing anybody else in?"

The central focus of my business was always to accommodate the agents' needs. I consider myself a Ph.D. in common sense, and common sense says you should treat people like they walk on water. Pretty soon I had three or four agents on board and more coming in all the time. Our motto was that we were a company built by agents, for agents, to better serve our customers. I believe that if you take care of your agents and treat them like they were your own customers, everybody wins because your agents will have the ability to do whatever is necessary to accommodate their customers. All of the other real estate firms were trying to impress the buyers and the sellers while overlooking the needs of their agents, so it wasn't surprising that agents left other companies to work with me.

Van C. Deeb Realtors became a five-person agency while I was still working out of my house. My home was on one of the busiest intersections in Omaha, and I had a small office with a separate entrance so the other agents could come in and make copies and drop off paperwork without interrupting me. The office was probably only 200 square feet, but having an office attached to my house was convenient and helped keep my overhead low while eliminating the need to constantly get a babysitter for my daughter.

I wanted to put a Van C. Deeb Realtors sign in my front yard to help get my name out in the community. My house was next to a public library and across the street from a restaurant, so it was not embedded in a residential neighborhood. My challenge was to convince the Permits Department of the City of Omaha to let me put a sign in my yard. I hired a company to make an architectural drawing. It was going to be a nice, classy sign with landscaping around it, no bigger than 3 by 5 feet.

Six people were on the board of the Permits Department, and five of them approved my request without a hitch. The sixth person was one of my competitors whose family had started their real estate business in 1857. He "recused" himself, which meant he abstained from voting on my sign request because we were in the same industry and he was a competitor. At that time my company had only five agents and his company had several hundred, but apparently he had the foresight to realize that we would eventually hurt his business if he did anything to help us out. (As it turned out later, he was right!)

I needed unanimous approval from the Permits Department to put up my sign, which meant that my request was denied. Making this outcome even more difficult to swallow was the fact that I had referred several new agents to that firm. At that time brand new agents had started to call and ask about working for my company, but since we were still a small agency and I was not yet prepared to train people because I was too busy, I would tell them to go visit this other company and join them to get started in the industry. Thank God we started training new agents within a year or two, and boy did we train! They became incredible, highly respected Realtors.

Since I couldn't put a sign up on my property, I decided to rent office space. Agents started coming to work for Van C. Deeb Realtors because they liked our policies. We ended up changing the name to DEEB and Associates and eventually to DEEB Realty. Our commission split was the best in the real estate business, with the agent receiving the majority of the commission instead of only half of it. We made sure our agents received all the leads from their own listings, and we paid commission checks the same day as the closing instead of making them wait for several days.

A couple of years passed and our company grew to 25 or 30 agents. I was introduced to a gentleman who was impressed with the way we did business. He said, "You need to get the word out. Let the city of Omaha know that you have the best commission program in the industry and you have a philosophy that lets agents be the true independent contractors that they are, with the full support that you give them as a broker." He asked me, "Where do you want to take this company?" I had never really thought about growing it quickly. My attitude had always been "if we grow, great, but if we don't, that's fine with me," because I was out there listing and selling properties myself, along with our agents.

This gentleman decided to come on board our company full-time, and his job was to get the word out. He stayed for two years, and he put us on the map. By the time he left we had about 100 agents.

At that point we were still using a 1200-square-foot office space with only one bathroom. We were on top of each other in there, and we were using metal desks that I had bought for $100 each. Competing firms would always tell their agents, "Why would you want to go to DEEB Realty? Have you seen their office?" It was not a classy place, yet we had agents joining us left and right because of the way we treated people.

In 2002 we decided to look for bigger offices. It took a year to find the perfect office building. I put an offer on it and got the building. It was occupied by tenants, so we had to wait until March of 2003 for the tenants to move out. It was a beautiful office building—7500 square feet, Corian® countertops in the bathrooms, incredible woodwork, and gorgeous conference rooms—so now all of a sudden our competitors could no longer think of anything to say that would deter their agents from joining us. DEEB

Realty had it all: the best commission program, the best philosophy on how to treat agents, and an incredibly beautiful office building. Then we opened up a branch office in Sarpy County, so we had two locations.

In 2008, DEEB Realty was involved in one out of every four real estate transactions that happened in the Omaha metro area, which includes Council Bluffs

Deeb Realty attributes growth to agent-friendly atmosphere

by Stephanie Critser

Although owner Van Deeb's goal isn't for Deeb Realty to be the biggest player in town, the residential — and sometimes commercial, as requested — real estate agency has grown to rank as the fourth largest Omaha firm in volume and one of the Chamber of Commerce 25 fastest growing companies.

The 10-year-old agency began with just Deeb and now has 115 agents. A new office was purchased in April at 2611 S. 117th St. to accommodate the staff.

"We've grown because of the way we compensate real estate agents," Deeb said. "We empower them with flexibility and the ability to negotiate fees with customers.

"Customers have become more educated and realize that the real estate company has very little to do with success in buying or selling homes. The companies don't do that, the agents do.

"Even though we're a full-service agency, we give agents the ability to do what they have to do to get the deal."

Deeb said the company philosophy is to accommodate all realtors' needs and wants, making them among the highest paid so they in turn will serve customers better.

"I modeled the firm after firms on the East and West coasts," he said. "Most agents are held back by corporate needs and wants, but here each agent feels he owns the company.

"We want agents to make as much as they can without the company dipping into their profits, so our agents don't have monthly fees. Our commission structure enables agents to sell one house versus two or three houses and make the same amount of money as many agents elsewhere."

Ninety percent of real estate agents get out of the business within their first two years, Deeb said.

"Often, they are not trained properly and lose motivation, which is why training has become important to us and we offer more than 120 training courses a year," he said. "Because of our hands-on one-on-one personal training, we have a 98 percent retention rate of new agents.

"Our No. 1 goal is to be recognized as the best place in town for agents to work. We don't have a recruiting coordinator, so all of the agents who have come to join us have done so by word of mouth. We had 100 agents in our former 1,000-square-foot office, and I think that speaks volumes about what we do for agents."

The new 7,500-square-foot facility be-

tween Center and Arbor Streets is in a great location for agents, Deeb said.

"It was really designed for agents," he said. "It has an agents' computer room, a resource room, conference areas and private rooms.

"The central location gives agents access to all areas of Omaha, especially growing areas like the northwest and southwest."

Deeb Realty takes an active approach in giving back to the community, sponsoring athletic programs for Millard North High School, Burke High School, the University of Nebraska at Omaha and the city of Bellevue's youth programs as well as an annual scholarship at Burke High.

"It's expensive for parents today to pay for kids' sports," Deeb said. "We try to eliminate a lot of costs for the parent.

"The last thing we want to see is a kid who wants to play and can't because his parents can't afford it. We try to encourage each agent to give back to the community because it is the community that has made us successful. It only makes sense to support those who support us."

Deeb was born in Omaha and graduated from Burke High School. He played football at UNO while earning a marketing degree.

"I went into real estate right after college graduation," he said. "I knew I wanted to get into a sales field with big high-ticket rewards.

"I was in real estate for 11 years before starting my own company. I thought Omaha was in desperate need of a company that was more agent-oriented. I needed more flexibility to spread my wings as an agent and thought others would too."

A single father of a 15-year-old girl, Deeb enjoys motivational speaking as a hobby and wrote a book about building customer relationships, "Selling From the Heart."

He has been on the athletic board of UNO for 11 years and was UNO's man of the year in 2000 for his contributions to the school. He was inducted into Burke High School's Hall of Fame in 2002 for his community contributions.

A member of the Omaha Board of Realtors, the National Association of Realtors and the Nebraska Association of Realtors, he was once ranked in the top 300 house salesmen by National Realtor magazine.

"This business is great for someone who is motivated and success-driven," Deeb said. "I get a real thrill out of seeing an average salesman become great."

Deeb in front of the new office location ... "We've grown because of the way we compensate real estate agents."

and surrounding communities in western Iowa. We had over 300 agents when I sold the company in late January of 2009. In addition to our philosophy of accommodating agents' needs, I attribute our success to two other factors: community outreach and choosing the right people.

Community Involvement, Effective Leadership Pay Off

Instead of hiring an agency, we created all of our own ads and marketing strategies. One of my best marketing ideas was our T-shirt campaign. Every time DEEB Realty sponsored a youth program, we provided T-shirts for all the kids on the team. The shirt might have their school name on the front, but it had our big DEEB Realty logo on the back. Soon there were thousands of DEEB Realty T-shirts all over our city. You couldn't go into a grocery store without seeing a kid wearing one of our shirts.

The T-shirt campaign turned out to be the best form of advertising we could have done, because it showed our support for Omaha area youth while spreading our name throughout the community in a positive way. For example, one of our agents told me, "Thank you for sponsoring Keystone Little League last year. I got a listing and they didn't even know who I was, but when I called them they immediately went with me because we had sponsored their kid's team."

Another factor in our success was having the right people on board at the right time. One was the gentleman who helped put us on the map, and another was our General Manager who put us on the globe and then some. He started out at DEEB Realty by answering phones and doing administrative work, gradually moved into an assistant manager position and then a manager position, and eventually became our General Manager.

In the real estate industry, usually no more than 70 percent of the people in a firm really like the manager. It's rare for a manager to win everybody over, but this gentleman did. Everybody in the company had great things to say about him. He ended up buying the firm from me in late January of 2009, and it was a very smooth transition. I have always described him as a "Gift from God," and he is!

"People First" Culture Promotes Steady Growth

DEEB Realty takes a common sense approach that accommodates the needs of agents, supports their development, and keeps them motivated along the way. As a result, they rarely leave. One of our competitors always seems to have about 420 agents. Each year about 70 new agents join them and another 70 leave, so the total number stays the same. By contrast, our company kept growing.

DEEB Realty offers training classes in every aspect of real estate to help agents become better at what they do. When we started offering classes, nobody else was providing that kind of training. It is also a great place for people to hold their license, because there are no costs except for their board fees or Multiple Listing Service fees. In addition, we have never required agents to make their customers pay the add-on fees that were routinely charged by other firms. Agents hated making their customers pay those fees, and they were glad to come to a firm that didn't make them do that.

An important part of DEEB Realty's "People First" culture has been to look toward the future instead of focusing on our past accomplishments. We never said, "Wow, did you see what kind of month we had?" or "Look how big we've become" or "Look at all the agents who are leaving our competitors to join DEEB Realty." We didn't gloat about our success— we just kept moving forward.

The same competitors who tried to discourage me from starting a new real estate company back in 1993 came back a few years later and offered to buy us out. We kept these offers quiet because we didn't want our agents or anyone outside the company to think we were interested in selling to one of our competitors.

> *Take the high road. Truth, honesty, and hard work will prevail in the long run.*

Several competing firms tried to keep us from growing in the early years by using tactics that were unethical, unfair, and not true, but truth and honesty and hard work prevailed in the long run and the level of respect that we eventually received from our competitors stood in sharp contrast with the way we had been treated before. We've also seen the other real estate firms adopt many of the same practices that we initiated back in 1993. We revolutionized the way real estate companies operate in Omaha.

I believe the most effective form of leadership is to lead by example. You have to show people that you care about them, and that means listening to their needs and wants, maybe going off structure and policy sometimes to accommodate them, and making sure they have a fun environment to work in. I don't believe you should ever take anyone for granted, so I always made a point of thanking everybody who worked in the office each day before they left.

> *Always treat people the way you would want to be treated.*

However, reflecting back, I still don't think I thanked my General Manager and staff enough for what they did for the firm.

Respect and consideration have always been an important aspect of DEEB Realty. We never treated Top Producers as if they were better than everybody else. All of the agents had access to the manager and to me. Nobody was too good or too busy to spend time with somebody who was just getting started.

The agents at DEEB Realty have been the best mouthpiece we've had because they absolutely love working for the company. People who came over from our competitors would tell us, "The only thing I regret is not coming to DEEB Realty sooner."

We did a lot of things right, but our number one asset was treating people fairly and with respect. Full-time agents make it their life to be successful in real estate, so the last thing DEEB Realty wanted to do was to hinder that. We wanted to make our agents' experience of working at our firm so wonderful that it made their jobs much easier. We followed a very old rule based on common sense—treat people the way you would want to be treated—and it paid big dividends.

6A   OMAHA WORLD-HERALD   SATURDAY, JANUARY 24, 2009   OMAHA.COM

Deeb Realty founder sells his company to employee

By Christine Laue
WORLD-HERALD STAFF WRITER

Deeb Realty founder and owner Van Deeb is selling his company — one of Omaha's largest real estate firms — to employee Andy Alloway.

Alloway will keep the Deeb Realty name and culture, Deeb said Friday.

"I am not retiring," Deeb, 49, said. "I'm just going down a different path of motivational speaking across the country."

Deeb

Deeb said the company has never been for sale, although competitors have offered to buy it in the past. He started crafting his exit strategy about two years ago, planning all the while for Alloway, the company's general manager, to take over.

Alloway started at Deeb Realty in 2000 doing administrative work, has worked as an assistant manager and has served as general manager since 2003.

"I've never seen a man that has more respect from the entire company and its associates," Deeb said. "Andy and I are both extremely excited."

Deeb started in real estate when he was 21 and formed Deeb Realty out of his garage when he was 34, working as its only agent. Today the firm has 350 agents.

"So I'm a big fan of starting something from nothing, and I want to go preach that to the world — that anybody can do anything they set their mind to."

After several years of motivational speaking "on a hobby basis," he decided he wanted to do it on a professional level and recently formed Sellabration Seminars.

"I didn't want to wait much longer. I couldn't be effective and do both," he said of the two businesses. "This is a good time for me to concentrate on the speaking end."

Deeb declined to disclose the sale price.

The sale was finalized Friday afternoon, Deeb said. His last day at Deeb Realty will be Jan. 30, he said.

■ **Contact the writer:**
444-1183, christine.laue@owh.com

2 Selling from the Heart

It's no accident that the title of this chapter is the same as the title of my first book. I still believe strongly in selling from the heart. Why? Because it's what sales is all about. We have all heard the advice "Don't sell from your head, sell from your heart" and one of my favorites, "People don't care how much you know until they know how much you care."

When you advise people based on what your heart tells you is the right thing to say, your customer benefits. And when you're in sales, your customer's concerns and needs are your responsibility. Tell them the right thing—the way you feel from your heart. Believe me, it really does work.

What Is Sales?

What is sales, and what sort of person is most successful at selling? Of course, the old cliché that says everyone is selling something is certainly true. No doubt at some time each of us has been in a position of trying to persuade another that we should be hired or given a raise, or that our opinion is the right one. However, this book is written for people whose primary job is to sell something—individuals who derive compensation from convincing customers to buy a product or service from them instead of buying it from their competitors. I know that anyone who will apply the principles in this book can have a very successful sales career.

> *Find a way to love your job and it won't seem like work.*

What does it mean to be successful in sales? For me, there are two distinct rewards. Making a high income is the first. IRS statistics show that 1 percent of Americans are considered wealthy. Of that 1 percent, 74 percent own their own business, 10 percent are in professions like medicine and law, and 5 percent are in sales. The remaining 1 percent are entertainers or professional athletes. It is obvious that for those of us who don't fit into the other categories, the way to earn a higher income is through sales.

The greater reward, I believe, is not an accumulation of wealth but an accumulation of friends (relationships). The relationships built throughout a career based on helping people are invaluable and longer-lasting than material wealth.

I chose to include the word *heart* in the title of this chapter because my conviction about my ability comes from the heart. I believe that people understand what is in my heart. Their recognition of my sincerity is what separates me from the rest of the sales pack. I intend to show you how to put your heart into sales so you can also separate yourself from the pack. The most important thing I want to communicate is that this separation doesn't start with the sales presentation. It begins when you greet the first person you see or talk to during the day, every day!

Networking and selling from the heart means that we treat everyone with respect and interest. We operate in a positive environment all the time. People are drawn to positive, sincere people. Become the kind of person others want to spend time with. This will pay enormous

> *If people are sure about your motives, they'll be sure about your product.*

dividends in terms of your attitude, your relationships, and certainly, your career. Sales leaders face the same challenges of maintaining a positive attitude and a friendly manner as their less successful counterparts. The difference is that they find a way to be pleasant. They take advantage of opportunities instead of letting daily challenges turn their attitudes sour. They understand that planting the seeds of respect, interest, and accommodation reaps a harvest of trust.

What is your reaction when someone makes you feel that you are not important enough to include in a conversation, or that your views are not significant enough to be considered? Sales leaders know that everyone wants to feel important—to be treated with interest and respect. This makes the other person feel comfortable. When people are at ease in your presence they will be open and direct about their needs. Accordingly, your responsibility as a sales professional is to make all customers feel that no one could fulfill their requirements and provide the service as efficiently and with as much sincere interest as you can. Toward that end, a real pro treats all contacts as if they are part of the sales process, and people know that they can expect to receive attention and consideration in all their dealings with that sales professional.

If you aspire to high achievement in sales, one of your most important attributes will be an unconditional belief in and a real love for your product or service. When you love what you're presenting, your enthusiasm and excitement will be genuine and your emotional appeal will be very persuasive. By the same token, if your personality lacks that spark, the appeal is less emotionally compelling. The best and most effective sales presentations are those that convey passion and heartfelt conviction about the product or service.

When I talk with prospective home buyers, I always make sure they understand how committed I am to this industry and how pleasurable it will be to leave no stone unturned in my quest to meet their home-buying needs. I want to ensure they are completely satisfied and eager to recommend me to their friends. I give my commitment orally and in writing, but I also show by my conduct that I can't wait to get started. My customers are confident that my efforts on their behalf will be untiring because I love what I'm doing.

Often I am asked to speak to groups of students. I always recommend that young people begin working on their career while they're still in school. They should take steps that will help establish them as future leaders in their fields by joining special interest groups in school, performing volunteer work in the community, and participating in extracurricular activities.

Teachers should encourage their students to begin considering vocational options during high school. A student who decides on a sales career should definitely focus on product or service groups of interest. Toward that end, the student should research industries and companies either for class projects or for extra credit.

Ambitious students will want to be in a position of choosing companies they would like to work for instead of interviewing aimlessly, without a specific goal or useful knowledge. I can confidently state that progressive companies will want to hire entry-level candidates who have done their homework. Those who come to the interview armed with background information about the specific company and the industry will be impressive. That type of preparation gives the candidate leverage and control that the average interviewee doesn't have. This is the first step that a young sales pro can take to pull ahead of the pack.

Confidence is another result of solid preparation, and this confidence enables sales pros to give their presentations to customers at all levels. The ability to feel comfortable and confident when presenting to the CEO as well as the purchasing agent is crucial.

Is there such a thing as a natural salesperson? There's no doubt that certain people are more outgoing and driven to bringing others around to their point of view. This combination of personality traits certainly makes these people good candidates for sales careers. If you enjoy meeting new people and sharing your opinions with them, you will have an easier time prospecting and making cold calls than someone who doesn't have these traits. However, these attributes alone are not enough to ensure success in sales. If fact, if they are used incorrectly they can do more harm than good. It can be tedious to listen to people who love the sound of their own voice but have nothing of value to share with others.

If you have chosen a sales career and are concerned that you aren't extroverted enough, worry no more! Just being comfortable around people is a good place to start. Remember, a successful sales career is built on following the examples of people whose success you wish to duplicate. You can be sure that any sales leader you choose to emulate will have a winning strategy that combines goal setting, visualization, and discipline, as well as a belief in and a love for what they're doing and a commitment to long-term activity. This combination of practices is much more powerful than the efforts of a likable extrovert who relies solely on charm and persuasiveness.

Love of one's career provides a significant incentive to the aggressive pro. Those who face the day eager to engage in their chosen field attract success like a magnet. I often hammer this point home with the following statement: most people either don't like their jobs or would be happier doing something else, yet they still perform adequately or even well. Just imagine what they could achieve in a field they love! If you choose sales, be sure to sell something you are passionate about.

People ask me regularly if I think they would do well in sales. I can usually tell within a short time if they are good candidates. I look for the light in their eyes that tells me they are truly interested in the subject and what I have to say. I question them about their goals and comfort level around new people. When they answer and then ask a question, it's a pretty good sign that they have the raw talent and interest that will be necessary for a successful career. If they tell me there is one particular product or area of sales that is very appealing to them, I recommend they go for it. Notice that I didn't say that I look for a very outgoing person who loves to talk. I look for sincere interest, the inclination to listen intently and follow with a question, and attraction to a particular area of sales.

Another quality that is important for a sales professional is the ability to delay gratification. In some sales positions the commission may be paid several months after the actual sale. I have seen people quit a salaried position to try sales without considering the consequences of receiving delayed compensation. The shock of not being able to count on a regular check is discouraging at best. If you're leaving a salaried position to begin a sales career, be sure to factor in that possibility.

I guess it's pretty apparent what sales means to me. I have found that it provides enough personal and material rewards to appeal to the very best business people in the world. When done correctly, it results in happy, satisfied customers who have acquired something they needed, and who have become positive assets in our network of relationships. If also provides a substantial income that we have earned and of which we can be proud.

If you're considering sales or if you are already in sales and wondering if you belong, why not reflect on the following questions?

- Am I willing to set goals?

- Am I willing to set myself apart from the pack by my work habits?

- Am I willing to use rejection as an opportunity to analyze how to improve my presentations?

- Am I willing to delay gratification and make short-term sacrifices?

- Am I willing to make a long-term commitment to my field?

- Am I willing to tell customers I love my job?

- Am I willing to operate under the conviction that I control my own destiny?

- Am I willing to treat everyone the same all the time?

If your answer to these questions is a strong "YES," I promise you that the information in the following chapters will be more helpful than you ever dreamed.

I Believe. . .

My first book focused on how to achieve success by building relationships, setting goals, providing excellent customer service, and so on. I didn't mention my spiritual beliefs at that time because I wasn't as spiritually oriented then as I am today, even though I have always been a praying man. Throughout my career I have made a habit of thanking God daily for the many blessings I have received and praying for others to receive God's blessings as well. Over time, my faith in God has become a central part of my life, so I decided to include some of my beliefs in this chapter.

I was lucky to grow up in a family with a wonderful Christian heritage. My great-grandfather was a very well-known minister, and people would come from all over to hear him preach. We asked God to bless our food before almost every meal, and I was taught to pray at an early age every night before bed. We went to church every Sunday, at least until I got older and would only go when it was convenient for me and to make my mother happy. She loved it when I would show up at church and sit by her. I didn't take going to church very seriously; I fidgeted all the time while looking around the room to see if any of my friends or cousins were there so I could make faces at them and make them laugh. As time went on, I attended church with my family on holidays and again mostly to make my mother happy, and even though I was well into adulthood I still didn't take it as seriously as I should have.

One day I realized that my life had been a pretty enriched and enjoyable one with many great rewards, yet something was missing: I had not developed an understanding of God. I could recite the Lord's Prayer and sit in church and listen to the sermon and get something out of it, but I wanted more. I started visiting other churches to see if I could find one that met my requirements, although at that time I was a little vague as to what they were. I was searching for a missing part of my life, and I wasn't sure where to find it.

All my life I had continued to pray. Early in my sales career I remember coming home at night and thanking God for a great day of accomplishments. Not only did I pray at night but in my car in the morning and throughout the day.

I truly believe that you can be a great Christian without belonging to any church, but it helps if you can attend a church that teaches about God and how he works in our daily lives. Today, I feel like I have come closer to finding that church. I am very impressed by the minister, the Bible study, and the overall atmosphere. So after about three years of looking around, I believe I have found a church where I can learn more about God.

Speaking of what I believe, let me share with you a few core beliefs that have helped to shape my attitude and my business outlook. Some of these are spiritual and others are not, but I hope you will be able to incorporate many of them into your life or thought pattern:

- I believe if you build your life on a strong relationship with God and put his secrets into practice, you can have joy and peace even when things are not as you would like them to be.
- I believe God will help you rise above it all, and even your most difficult challenges can be overcome.

- I believe God will give you supernatural power and strength when circumstances are beyond your own ability. You can lean on him and ask for that power moment by moment.

- I believe God will provide you with the real sense of his presence in times of trouble. You will feel him there with you.

- I believe God will show you that he has a bigger purpose for you and your life than whatever you are going through and that your life is a long book that goes way past the chapter you are in.

- I believe that learning to understand others and trying very hard to consider their point of view and how they look at a situation will make you a better person.

- I believe my mother is the most understanding person I know (especially if you agree with her!). Talk about being a blessed man—I truly am, for God blessed my life by letting me be her son. She is one of the most enjoyable people I know to be around.

- I believe God will bring good out of even the worst things that occur. Adversity creates opportunity.

- I believe God will protect you and preserve you, even when bad things happen to you. He will keep you, if you let him in.

- I believe God will fill you with his love and peace in the midst of adversity and challenges, regardless of the situation you are experiencing.

- I believe God will guide you to have the answers you need for whatever you are going through.

- I believe God will open new doors as old ones close or bad events take them away. There is always a tomorrow with God.

- I believe that people who act like they are smarter than you usually are not, but it's always fun to feed their ego and make them feel like they are.

- I believe that education is important; I believe that people with all levels of degrees and designations are educated and disciplined people. As much as I respect education I would still rather do business with someone who has a Ph.D. in common sense. I believe that the smartest people in business are the ones with the most common sense. It's a bonus if someone is very well educated and also has common sense.

- I believe that people who are judgmental and critical of others are truly miserable themselves. I believe they are envious and jealous of the people they criticize. Leaders and overall happy people are usually the targets of these types of people. Stay away from them—far, far away—regardless of whether they happen to be friends, family members, or business associates. They will find a way to bring you down.

- I believe that when you see a man or woman in a military uniform, you should acknowledge them by thanking them or giving them something, even if it is just a smile.

> *Have you had joy in your life? Has your life brought joy to others? If the answer is "no" or "not always," remember it is never, ever too late.*

Recently I took my parents out to lunch and saw a table of four men in uniform sit down to eat. I went over to their table to thank them and gave them more than enough money to buy their lunch. They all stood up to thank me.

What a great feeling it is to do something so effortless for people who make so many sacrifices to protect our freedom. God bless our troops serving overseas and here in the United States!

Build Relationships

The days of salespeople as order-takers are over. Why? Because some other salesperson will go after your customers and try to build relationships with them while you are sitting around waiting for the phone to ring. Apparently you have been doing good business with your customers for a long time or you wouldn't still be getting their business, but today the most effective sales approach is different. Your competitors are finding success with a new and unique approach to sales—no hard sell, no gimmicks, simply building relationships.

Your goal should not be just to get the quick sale but to enhance your relationship with the customer by going above and beyond the call of duty and job description. I believe that instead of going after 500 prospects, it's better to concentrate on strengthening relationships by treating your current customers like gold. Rather than just calling and pitching your prospect on a product or service, for example, follow up on what you learned during your last visit or phone conversation. For example, he may have mentioned that he was getting ready for his daughter's high school graduation, so you will want to ask him how the graduation went. This kind of information should be kept in a customer or prospect file so you can personalize your conversation and make each individual feel important and valued.

Choose Your Words with Care

When you're talking with a prospect or customer, saying too much can talk you out of a sale. The best approach is to listen attentively and respond only if needed. Often your customer will make statements that don't require a response. There is no need to talk

> *Your thoughts become words, your words become actions, and your actions can make or break you. Think before you speak! Are your words going to offend anyone, or will they be productive not only in your own life but also for all who hear you?*

unless you are asked a question or need to shed some light on what your customer has said.

When you do respond, be sure your message is appropriate to what your customer is saying. No matter what you say, be honest. Don't try to mislead your way into a sale. If you're honest, you will never have to worry about talking to your customer two or three weeks down the road and trying to remember what you said the last time you talked with them.

Dare to Be Different

"When you can do all the common things in life in an uncommon way you will command the attention of the world." George Washington Carver

If you have spent any amount of time with me, you would probably agree that I am someone who thinks outside the box...way outside. I have never been one to follow the crowd. I separated myself from the pack early in my sales career and as a business owner by doing things that were unique and would grab people's attention: anything from flooding the market with my T-shirt campaign to sitting on the roof of a building to raise money for charity (both of which I discuss in other chapters).

People like to do business with people who are passionate about what they do. If you do things differently, it shows them your creativity and ability to accomplish a goal without going down the normal, boring path that a lot of other people in your industry will travel.

I like—no, let me rephrase that—I LOVE being considered a maverick in my industry. I LOVE it when people say that my company revolutionized the way real estate companies operate. We changed the industry by doing things in a different way that benefits everyone involved: the customers, the public, and most of all the associates of the firm. I know it sounds amazing, and I was not too popular with my competitors in my industry, but treating our associates like they own the company and accommodating their needs is what made us unique and different. Think about ways you can "Dare to be Different" in your own industry. There's a good chance that every life you touch will benefit greatly.

Strengths Versus Weaknesses

Ready for some homework? Good, because you're about to get some. Use the diagram on page 37, or make one on a separate sheet of paper. Start by making a list of your weaknesses. For example, your list might look like the following:

1. Cold calling
2. Giving presentations
3. Returning phone calls from upset customers right away

You may need to take a day or two to complete your list. Once you've finished identifying your weaknesses, do the same thing with your strengths. Be honest with yourself. You are the only one who has to see this list, unless you want to get an opinion from a friend, co-worker, or manager. If so, let that person look over your list. If you haven't been able to identify any strengths, you aren't being fair to yourself. Think a little harder.

Acknowledge your weaknesses and work to overcome them. You are not necessarily trying to turn a weakness into a strength. You just want to find a way to eliminate the weakness so it doesn't hold you back.

When you look at your strengths, try to identify something about yourself that is different and unique—something that makes you stand out from the crowd. Spend time finding your niche. Make sure it is something you really enjoy doing. Incorporate it into your sales program. Don't forget you are selling from the heart. You are real, not phony. Real people have a variety of interests, and it's okay for your sales presentation to reflect your uniqueness.

Weaknesses	Strengths

Deeb & Associates Real Estate

Firm takes maverick approach to residential market

Van C. Deeb, owner of Deeb & Associates Real Estate, is taking a maverick approach to the Omaha area market with his two-year-old firm.

"My focus is not on how big our company will become, and I'm not seeking additional agents," Deeb said. "I'd rather work with 75 customers a year and make them the happiest in town."

Deeb said his firm seeks to fill a niche as a small, strongly service-oriented advocate for each of its customers.

Deeb & Associates has six agents, who work out of their residences. The firm's office, in a house at 406 N. 90th St., is used largely for meetings and signing transaction documents.

After graduating from UNO in 1981 with a degree in marketing, the former outside linebacker attended a real estate specialty school in Dallas. During 12 years in

Deeb

the Dallas-Fort Worth market Deeb rose from rookie homebuilding salesman to one of the state's top realtors.

He was ranked top rookie producer in the state of Texas one year and for two consecutive years was Dallas' top sales volume producer. He sold $19 million one year and topped that figure by more than $1 million the next year.

Deeb said discipline and a focused work ethic helped him achieve significant success as a young agent.

"I've learned to use every ounce of my energy in marketing homes," Deeb said. "It starts with an immediate callback in response to a customer and consistently going above and beyond the call of duty. Too many times a sign is just stuck in

a yard with the hope that somebody sells the property."

Deeb said he finally gave in to his parents' coaxing and returned to his hometown in 1993, he brought with him some pretty well honed ideas on how he would differentiate Deeb & Associates from the competition.

"I tell my agents we're going to cater to our customers' time schedules and that they had better be prepared to be inconvenienced," Deeb said. "We encourage inspections of our homes prior to sale, so that two weeks later the buyer isn't finding something wrong."

When customers visit Deeb & Associates' office, they can discuss business in the dining room while their children play or watch videos in the living room.

Deeb said his customer-first attitude causes him to stay strictly within the price range set by those seeking to buy.

"I frequently hear our customers say that agents from other companies have shown them houses above the price range they've identified, and many times an agent will show more of his company's listings so that he will make more money," Deeb said.

He said he's never been reticent about separating himself from the rest of the pack.

"From my viewpoint, the days of the 7 percent listing are
Continued on next page.

Deeb takes maverick approach to residential market

Continued from preceding page.

gone," Deeb said. "The listing commission we worked with in Dallas was 5 or 6 percent."

He said the focus of Deeb & Associates is to build long-term customer relationships rather than seek the quick sale.

His firm hit $10 million in sales last year, and sales were up 9 percent during the first quarter of this year. The average selling price is $150,000 to $175,000.

"Although our favorite area is west Omaha, we have listings from Florence to Gretna and homes priced from $20,000 to $500,000," Deeb said.

One of Deeb's customers had called an old high school buddy who was a residential sales agent and asked to see houses in the $80,000 range. He was told he couldn't be shown property in that low a price range. He then called Deeb.

"There is no excuse for that kind of treatment," Deeb said. "I believe the best real estate agents in town are the ones who listen, understand the customers' needs and then perform accordingly."

When Deeb is touring a house for a prospective listing, he gives the owner a pad and pen and asks him to take notes in each room. Paint touchups, furniture placement and lighting are all items which are recorded.

"Our last seven listings have sold within three days," Deeb said. "One of my customers had already moved out of the house she wanted to sell, and it looked like a morgue. I had her bring some of the furniture back in and put soap in the soap dishes and towels on the towel racks. By making the house look fresh, we were able to sell it in two weeks for more than she had planned to ask.

"It's important to create excitement with a listing. We'll put a sign out on Thursday, fax the listing to 30 or 40 real estate offices and make the Sunday afternoon open house create the excitement of the grand opening of a store."

Deeb said such enthusiasm has come naturally to him ever since he was in second grade and was named king of Mount View Elementary School's annual carnival for selling the most tickets.

"The only way I will take a listing is if it's a salable listing," Deeb said.

He was the second agent to give a young couple living near 69th and Maple an estimate on the value of their home. Deeb's figure was $8,000 higher than the one given by the competitor.

"We sold it within 30 days and made them $6,500 more than they had been prepared to sell it for," Deeb said. "That gave them more money to put into their new home."

He said 97 percent of his business last year was from referrals from previous customers.

"One customer has referred 11 people to me," Deeb said. "I take them to Lone Star or the restaurant of their choice after they give me a referral."

He said he likes to go in person to deliver the check to each seller.

"The number one thrill for me personally is when I can get them more than they expected for their house," he said.

He said it's been difficult to adjust to the level of respect that real estate brokers get in Omaha compared to what he experienced in Texas.

"They treat you with high regard and as a real professional in Texas," Deeb said. "What we have to work on here is the public perception of our work."

He cited a recent survey by Realtor Today, a publication of the National Association of Realtors, which reported that only 4 percent of Americans view real estate agents as true professionals.

"The answer for us is to demand better training and higher ethical standards," he said.

Deeb, 36, is active in the UNO Beef Club and Maverick Club and the upcoming Children's Miracle Network benefit for Children's Hospital.

—RDB

Most salespeople put on their sales hat when they go to work. Try to incorporate your sales (helping) attitude into all of your everyday interactions.

3 Sell Them on You First

To be successful in a sales career, you must be able to engender in other people the belief that you will fulfill their legitimate need for a product or service with more professionalism and deeper interest in their benefit than any other person or company.

How do you do this? Before you try to sell a product or service to anyone, you must sell them on *you* first. It all begins with a sincere commitment to helping others. As I mentioned in Chapter 2, "People don't care how much you know until they know how much you care."

I believe—and I want to convince my customers to trust—that I will do a better job for them than any of my competitors—period!

The two key words here are *believe* and *trust*. I believe in myself, my product or service, my work ethic, and my sales ability. Because of the confidence that goes along with these beliefs, customers are compelled to trust me and my professional judgment. These elements of belief and trust are necessary for building and maintaining business relationships.

The STOYF Principle: Sell Them On You First

The most important principle in sales is what I call the STOYF Principle: Sell Them On You First. It's nothing fancy—just plain common sense.

Do you know anyone who would be eager to do business with someone they dislike? Others may disagree with me, but I truly believe that customers do business with people, not products. Have you ever heard someone say, "Give Mike a call if you're looking for a new copier; he's really a rotten person"? Not likely. We always hear people say, "Give Sue a call. She will take good care of you." Referrals will happen naturally if you take care of your customers.

People prefer to buy products and services from people they like. You must sell them on *you* before you try to sell them anything else.

Be Humble, Yet Confident

What type of attitude creates the strongest connection between salespeople and customers? I've found that the best approach is to be humble, yet confident. A lot of salespeople think being confident means acting cocky, but many potential customers are turned off by this type of attitude. I know this is true because I used to be that way. As a real estate salesperson I probably got away with it more easily than in most sales jobs, but I did better after I got rid of the cockiness.

Customers like to give their business to humble people. You can be the most confident person around and still be humble. Instead of trying to impress people by acting as though you are important, put your customer first. Mary Kay Ash, founder of Mary Kay Cosmetics, recognized this when she said, "Pretend that every single person you meet has a sign around their neck that says, 'Make me feel important.' Not only will you succeed in sales, you will succeed in life."

Make it clear that you are willing to work hard to understand and meet the needs of each client. People like to give business to someone who wants to do a good job.

There's no "one size fits all" approach to sales. Some people enjoy a talkative salesperson, but with others you will need to tone it down. With a more logical decision maker such as an accountant or banker, keep a low profile. I'm not saying you shouldn't be enthusiastic or confident, but this type of decision maker is less impressed with emotion than with logic.

You Are Your Own Worst Enemy

Have you ever said or done something and then regretted it later? Throughout my childhood, my mother often told me, "You are your own worst enemy." She didn't make this remark in a negative or critical tone of voice; instead, she just wanted to encourage me to think before acting. Of course she was 100 percent right. When I look back, I can see that anything good that has graced my life has happened mostly because of my own doing, and the same is true of the bad things that have happened to me.

As an adult, I experienced the truth of "You are your own worst enemy" more than once—usually because I did something on impulse instead of thinking about it first.

I encourage you to evaluate every important decision in your life or career before you do it. Sleep on it, think about it. Don't act without thinking. Life is challenging enough without fighting with yourself.

One of the many things I learned from my General Manager at DEEB Realty is the 24-hour rule: Think about a situation for at least 24 hours and then decide on your course of action. He was so right, because my response the next day was always completely different from what it would have been at that moment. Unfortunately I didn't always take his advice, and I suffered the consequences of acting immediately instead of waiting.

One of my past associates always used to say, "There is no such thing as a real estate emergency," and I agree. You don't need to deal with a situation without proper thought and action.

Don't be your own worst enemy. You will have plenty of those anyway, especially if you are a leader in your industry.

You Must Believe in Your Product or Service

If you want to maximize your success, you must believe in your product or service. You must be passionate about the benefits you can deliver to your customer.

If you are not passionate about your product or service, you have two choices: you can find another product to sell, or you can educate yourself into loving your product. Notice that I didn't say *liking* it; I said *loving* it. This may sound a little extreme, but it works!

Think about it this way: *if you do not think your product is the best and love to talk about it, how are you going to convince someone else that this is true?* If you are not excited or enthusiastic about what you are selling, your customer will be just as lukewarm as you are.

While I was driving to work one day, I noticed that the license plate holder on the car in front of me said, "Work sucks." I tried to get a glimpse of the driver so I could see what kind of person would have this attitude about work. If one of my employees drove a car to work with this slogan on it, I'd want to know why he had such a negative mindset. If a salesperson drove up in this car for an appointment with me, I would wonder why this person hated his job. That salesperson would be less likely to make the sale.

When you go into a situation with a negative mindset, you can expect a negative outcome. Luckily, the reverse is equally true: thinking positive goes a long way toward creating a positive outcome.

On Stage

Being in sales is a lot like being on stage. You're in the spotlight, just as an actor would be. Actors must rehearse and prepare to get the part. Once they do, they must maintain that level of performance or they will lose the part to someone else.

I believe sales is similar. Before you make a sales call, you need to prepare and rehearse. And once you've got someone's business, don't slack off. Always give your customers your best effort. Don't **take them for granted.**

> *You must think and act like a Top Producer if you are going to be a Top Producer.*

Why is it so important to prepare and rehearse? First impressions count. That's what this is all about: the first impression you make on people. Actors compete with a number of others each time they try out for a part, just as you compete with other salespeople for that customer's business.

If you don't make a good first impression, the person in charge of auditions is not going to call you back. Therefore, you need to treat each sales call as if it will be your only opportunity to sell the prospect.

After you get the business, treat each follow-up appointment as if it were your first audition. It is easy to become complacent and allow your level of service to slip over time. I have been guilty of that myself. If you don't maintain a high level of service, you will lose that customer to someone else.

Reverse the Role

One thing I like to do before I go on a sales call is talk to myself in the car. I practice what I'm going to say and prepare myself. In addition to the preparation I've already done, I like to reverse roles with my prospective customer in my own mind so I can be sure to treat others the way I would want to be treated.

I believe you will always be successful if you can reverse roles with your customers and see things through their eyes. Try to understand what is most important to your customers. As you talk with them, try to find out what their needs are and ask them what they expect from you.

> *Your ears are the most important part of your sales presentation.*

Be sure to listen carefully to what your customers are saying instead of making assumptions. If you find out what is important to your customers, you will have a better chance of getting their business.

How Much Do You Want Success?

I believe it is better to be alone than to hang around with negative people. A negative person is someone who either doesn't support you and understand your goals or someone who feels the need to find the downside in everything. You can't remain positive and optimistic when you surround yourself with pessimistic people.

Stay away from negative influences.

I enjoy being around people I can learn from—not just about business, but about life. These are the winners: not only those who are always number one in the company or first in everything, but those who are honest, big-hearted, interesting, and continually trying to improve themselves. These people look for the positive aspects of every situation and are not bitter about life. They are people you can trust and confide in. These are the people you want to include in your circle of influence.

The most important thing to remember is that sales is an individual effort. It is up to you to maintain a positive attitude. No one else can make you successful and give you a good attitude. Surrounding yourself with positive people can make it much easier to maintain your attitude than spending time with negative people.

Attitude is contagious! Speaking from experience, if I have a rotten attitude and spend time around friendly people, it's not long before I notice my attitude changing and becoming more positive. By the same token, misery loves company. Avoid being around negative people, because they will bring you down. If your peers or others in your office are negative, limit the amount of time you spend with them. Be sure to get positive support from others who are not in your immediate work environment. Create a balance of positive people in your life.

It can be challenging to maintain a positive attitude in sales because you are going to face rejection. Keep reminding yourself that you are not alone. Everyone faces rejection at one time or another. If you find yourself getting down or frustrated, it is up to you to bring yourself out of it. Call someone close for some insight into your situation. That person may give you a whole new way to look at your predicament.

Focus on the goals you have established. Let them be an inspiration to keep you moving forward during down periods. This gets into how badly you want to succeed. If you do not feel motivated by your goals, then read or re-read the discussion of goal-setting in Chapter 5 and re-evaluate your goals. You must set goals that reflect a strong desire to succeed. If you want the reward badly enough, you will do the work required to get there.

> *No method of achieving success will work unless YOU do.*

Keep your goals in front of you. Put sticky notes in your car, on the refrigerator door, and on your bathroom mirror. The most successful salespeople are the ones who create a motivating environment for themselves by keeping their goals visible constantly.

Don't think you have to be successful before you can have a good attitude and a strong desire for prosperity. Act as if you are already successful by adopting the habits of other leaders. I keep a reminder of this on my wall. It is a quote from Vince Lombardi that has to do with winning. It's called, "What It Takes to Be No. 1." I've adopted his words as my credo. Let me share them with you.

What It Takes to Be No. 1

Winning is not a sometime thing; it's an all the time thing. You don't win once in a while; you don't do things right once in a while; you do them right all the time. Winning is a habit. Unfortunately, so is losing.

There is no room for second place. There is only one place in my game, and that's first place. I have finished second twice in my time at Green Bay, and I don't ever want to finish second again. There is a second place bowl game, but it is a game for losers played by losers. It is and always has been an American zeal to be first in anything we do, and to win, and to win, and to win.

Every time a football player goes to ply his trade he's got to play from the ground up—from the soles of his feet right up to his head. Every inch of him has to play. Some guys play with their heads. That's O.K. You've got to be smart to be number one in any business. But more importantly, you've got to play with your heart, with every fiber of your body. If you're lucky enough to find a guy with a lot of head and a lot of heart, he's never going to come off the field second.

Running a football team is no different than running any other kind of organization—an army, a political party or a business. The principles are the same. The object is to win—to beat the other guy. Maybe that sounds hard or cruel. I don't think it is.

It is a reality of life that men are competitive and the most competitive games draw the most competitive men. That's why they are there—to compete. To know the rules and objectives when they get in the game. The object is to win fairly, squarely, by the rules—but to win.

And in truth, I've never known a man worth his salt who in the long run, deep down in his heart, didn't appreciate the grind, the discipline. There is something in good men that really yearns for discipline and the harsh reality of head to head combat.

I don't say these things because I believe in the "brute" nature of man or that men must be brutalized to be combative. I believe in God, and I believe in human decency. But I firmly believe that any man's finest hour, the greatest fulfillment of all that he holds dear, is that moment when he has worked his heart out in a good cause and lies exhausted on the field of battle—victorious.

—Vince Lombardi

Choose Your Friends Wisely

"He who walks with the wise grows wise, but a companion of fools suffers harm." (Proverbs 13:20) I love this proverb. It has the same meaning as "Don't flock with the turkeys if you want to soar with eagles." Are the people you associate with bringing you down? If they are, then move on. Maintaining a good attitude and a positive outlook on life can be lonely at times, because so many people are negative and they don't want anyone else to be happier or more successful than they are.

When I speak to high school students, I tell them how important it is to choose the people they spend time with. It's easy for young people to be influenced by the wrong crowd and end up doing things they would never do otherwise.

> *Fill your mind with positive thoughts. You can only be as successful as you think you can.*

In our current society it has become more and more of a challenge to understand someone's true motives in business and in pleasure. We all need to be careful with our associations at any stage in our lives.

Learn from Failure

Keep in mind that you are not a failure when things don't happen the way you planned. You only become a failure when you fail to try again.

Use past failures as stepping stones to victory, not as millstones around your neck. Learn from your mistakes and press forward with increased knowledge and experience.

Don't allow the fear of failure to keep you from moving ahead. You were put on this earth to be successful and victorious, and you are the only one who has the power to keep the dream that God has for you from coming true. God has given all of us everything we need to succeed, but it is up to us to make it happen.

God does not cause poverty or tragedy, but he can help us deal with it. He does not create negative circumstances to show you which way to go. He doesn't put hardships in your life just to teach you a lesson. God stands for love and wants all of us to develop the strength to overcome negativity, challenges, and hardships. He knows we can persevere.

Back to the Basics

When you feel frustrated because things aren't going the way you want them to, it's usually time to go back to the basics. When I was in my second and third years in real estate, I was among the Top Producers—the elite in real estate. Then all of a sudden things weren't going the way I wanted them to and I had to stop and ask myself, "What brought me to this level of achievement in the first place?" It wasn't being fancy or having the latest high-tech computer programs. I needed to go back to the basics—basic blocking and tackling. That's what got me back on track, and it will do the same for you. In real estate, it might mean making cold calls to for-sale-by-owners.

Often when you become a highly successful salesperson and you're doing many of the newest high-tech things, you may lose sight of the techniques that helped you be successful to begin with. You need to identify exactly what you were doing at the time when you first became successful.

If you are in a slump or not having the kind of year you want to have, it's never too late to turn it around. One nice thing about sales is that you can end that slump whenever you want. If you've been in a bad slump for the last two months, you can end it the day you decide to end it. Nobody can predict your sales for the next three months. You control your effort and performance, and you're the only one who can orchestrate your success.

You're never too far along in your career to go back to the basics. Let's say you've been in the business for the past 15 years and you're a Top Producer in your industry. You may tell yourself, "My gosh, I can't do what I used to do: knock on doors and make cold calls. That's what rookies do!" No, that's what people who want to be successful do!

Don't feel it's going to hurt your image if you need to go back to the basics to be successful. You'll probably impress your sales manager, especially if you're the one who mentions what you're doing wrong.

One of the best things about sales is that you can do the same success-building tasks over and over, updating them to suit the current times, and they will continue to work for you each time. I have done this several times during my career. I am the type of person who often seems to be going in a hundred different directions, and the only way to stop that is to go back and focus on what made me successful.

I refer to this as the Vince Lombardi philosophy. As a football coach, Lombardi was famous for his emphasis on the basics. Take a moment to think about this question: "What does it take to be No. 1?" No doubt you'll agree that going back to the basics is an important part of becoming the best you can be. (See pages 50–51 for the Vince Lombardi credo.)

More information at:
www.womensedition.com
visit our website

BUSINESS STYLE

Stacy Dryak is the first person I met at Deeb Realty's gorgeous new 7,500 sq. ft. office space, which opened in March of 2004. She's an extremely attractive, friendly, young lady who made me feel completely comfortable within 60 seconds after my arrival.

Van Deeb is the owner of Deeb Realty, which he told me is one of the largest real estate sales and brokerage companies in Omaha. His responsibilities include overseeing the entire operation and doing a "little bit of everything" in addition to being one of the company's talented six trainers. "What sets us apart," he said, "is how we train our agents to provide unequalled service in our industry."

Van got started in the real estate business in 1982 and opened his own business in 1993 working out of a 250 sq. ft. basement at his home in Candlewood. "I decided to open my own company," Van explained, "because of what I saw as limitations on the way agents could promote themselves. Agents are drawn to Deeb Realty because of our generous commission schedule, superior training and the fact that we have no monthly fees. Almost 90% of real estate agents get out of the business in their first two years. Our agents stay in because they're trained continually, and they can earn what they're worth."

According to a study Van showed me from recent Great Plains MLS (multiple listing service) statistics, Deeb Realty's average D.O.M. (days on market) was 34 as opposed to an average of 55 for the other leading local companies. The study reflected residential homes sold from 6/30/04 through 12/31/04 in Omaha, Bellevue and surrounding Nebraska communities.

"We aren't trying to be the largest real estate firm in Omaha," Van said, "But we do want to be the best. Agents want to work here because of our attitude. We want to be known for two things: (1) the best place for agents to work if they want to sell real estate in Omaha, and (2) the company that gives back to the community."

Van added, "I still sell real estate, only for family and friends, but I'm devoting most of my time to training agents. In 1996, I wrote Selling From the Heart, a book I distribute at speaking engagements. On Sundays from noon to 1:00 PM on 1290 KKAR Radio, I host How to Succeed in Business with Van Deeb."

He continued, "I do motivational speaking as a hobby. I get a thrill out of seeing an average salesperson become a great salesperson. If you have drive, determination and desire, there's nothing you can't do. Every person has greatness inside them, and I seem to have the ability to bring it out in people." His talents for motivating others and a stubborn streak propelled Van when he started his company. "I had the owners of two of the larger firms in Omaha tell me there wasn't room for another real estate company. If someone says, 'Van, you can't,' I'll say, 'Watch me.'"

"Everyone has greatness inside," he continued. "Sometimes it takes a little push to bring it out. I've lived my whole life off motivation. I even bought a house four blocks from theirs so I can eat lunch there every day."

Van mentioned that a past challenge he faced was educating customers to the fact that companies don't sell houses, agents do.

"We have 160 agents working here. Most of them have come from other local companies. I had to put many of them through detox because we're highly agent-oriented, and some of them were used to working in a corporate dictatorship environment. Agents want to work here because of our training. We provide at least 150 classes per year of free training and treat our agents like they're our customers."

Van's community contributions are focused on youth, particularly athletics. Deeb Realty sponsors the American Legion baseball team at Burke High School where he was recently inducted into the Hall of Fame. The company also sponsors baseball, football, basketball and volleyball at Millard North High School; the City of Bellevue's summer youth programs; and athletic programs at the University of Nebraska at Omaha where Van played football from 1977 to 1981.

DEEB REALTY
VAN DEEB
By Madelon Shaw

"It's expensive for parents to have their kids play sports," Van said. "Turning to corporate sponsors eliminates the need for car wash fund-raisers."

Raising his daughter, Courtney (now 16), by himself gave him an appreciation for the challenges parents face. "My daughter was born on my birthday so that was special," he said. "Here I had this healthy baby, but I knew several people around the same time who weren't as fortunate as I was, and I wanted to help, so I started raising money for Children's Hospital." For ten years he brought attention to Children's Hospital with his annual stint on the building's roof where he stayed until donors had contributed $10,000. He retired from roof sitting several years ago. "I'm actually afraid of heights," he said. "Now I'm using my energy in other areas."

Van shared his advice to others going into business for themselves: "Be honest and be motivated; have a passion for it or don't do it." He added that the rewards of his work include the consistent praise he receives from the community for what Deeb Realty is able to give back to them.

He shared some of his philosophies—toward customer service: "We treat customers as we'd want to be treated and have no tolerance for anything less." Toward work: "Make it fun. Life isn't a dress rehearsal. This is the real deal." Toward life in general: "It's a gift, and I'm taking advantage of every second."

A native Omahan and the youngest of five children, Van got a taste of sales early in life. "I knew I wanted to be in sales when I sold the most carnival tickets in second grade at Mount View Elementary," he said. "As an adult, I discovered that real estate is one of the biggest tickets you can sell." He added that his mother, Milly, who has an incredible personality, is his role model for being a good human being.

"Here at Deeb Realty," Van concluded, "We help with human development and do all we can to make sure our people achieve their goals and make sure they know that the best way to predict the future is to create it."

Deeb Realty is located at 2611 South 117th Street. Call (402) 491-0100 for an appointment and visit their website at deebrealestate.com. WE

Attracting New Clients

4

When I was a new real estate agent in Dallas, people used to ask me where I attracted all my customers. It was something I did on a daily basis because I had learned to treat every situation as a prospecting opportunity. I had also learned to overcome my reluctance to make cold calls on the phone or knock on the door of a prospect's home and introduce myself. New business will not come to you without any effort on your part—you will have to go out and get it by prospecting, cold calling, and networking.

Prospecting

One of the best ways to build your client base is by prospecting. This means reaching out to people you know as well as people your family, friends, and acquaintances know. In Dallas and later in Omaha, I used to tell everyone, "I sure would appreciate it if you would mention my name to anyone you know who is wanting to buy or sell a home." I would ask for referrals, while a less successful salesperson would sit back and say, "Well, I know that John, Mary, and Tim are aware that I'm in sales, and I'm sure they're going to tell somebody about me someday."

You must be willing to ask for help from people in your sphere of influence. Remind people that you are in business by making phone calls or sending personal notes on a regular basis. It may simply be a note wishing them "Happy Valentine's Day" written on your business letterhead or with your business card enclosed. Ideally, this type of contact should take place monthly, or at least quarterly. Consistency is the key!

Get involved in some type of community work, such as a church or charity group in which your family or friends participate. You can find a wealth of prospects there and at the same time be an asset to your community. If you don't have family or friends who are already involved in this type of organization, get involved on your own. Choose something that will be meaningful to you personally as well as professionally. Involvement in such a group increases your visibility, giving people a chance to get to know you.

> *"I'm a great believer in luck, and I find the harder I work, the more I have of it."* Thomas Jefferson

Get your name out there! When I started selling real estate in Dallas, I was away from family and friends so I had to build a new contact base from scratch. I did everything from stuffing my business cards in magazines at the grocery checkout stand to handing a card to anyone and everyone I saw. I used to go through 500 cards a month! Anytime there is an exchange of money between you and another person, that person should also have your business card. Everyone is a prospect! If they can't use your service at the moment, they may know someone who can. Prospecting doesn't always have to be by the book. Be creative!

Everyone you know should have some of your business cards, and you should also have theirs. The best approach to networking is one that is mutually beneficial. If you know someone who is an accountant, for example, tell them "If I can ever help you, I'd be thrilled to. Let me have some of your cards." Then give that person some of yours, and make a sincere effort to refer people who need their service.

Effective selling can't be done without networking, and repeat business can't be maintained without excellent customer service. You don't *ever* want to give your customers a reason to go somewhere else or tell their friends about one of your competitors. A study at Harvard University found that a satisfied customer will tell three other people about their experience, while a dissatisfied customer will tell seven others.

Working your current customer base is another form of prospecting. Let them know how important their satisfaction was at the time of the sale and how important it is now. Try to offer them something. For example, I offer all past and current customers my services as a Notary Public for an indefinite period of time at no charge. Becoming a Notary Public is a fairly easy process, the credential is inexpensive to maintain and adds to your credibility, and it allows you to provide something of value to your customers by saving them from having to make an extra trip to the bank. If they can see you and get something else done at the same time, they feel they've received a tremendous favor. Perhaps you can offer a special service like this.

When someone refers people to you, do something nice for them in return. I can recall several instances throughout my career in which one person gave me at least 10 referrals. When people gave me a referral, I used to take them out to dinner. At some point during the meal, I would say with great sincerity, "I want you to know how much I appreciate you referring Tom and Cindy to me, and if I can do anything for you, please let me know." A referral is the highest compliment you can receive from a customer!

Be creative and unique in your advertising. Look over ads from others in your field, and pull out the ones you like best. Analyze what elements catch your eye or grab your attention. Think about how your advertising can be unique. All of your advertising should reflect who you are and what you believe. If it comes from the heart, it will be unique.

To do effective prospecting, you need to surround yourself with people. If you want to be successful, you will integrate prospecting into every facet of your daily activity. Often people miss the meaning of prospecting and think it only has to do with cold calling. I have known salespeople who go through the day being discourteous to everyone they encounter, from the cashier at the convenience store to the waitress at the restaurant. Then they turn on the charm for that one- or two-hour period when they are prospecting on the phone. If you treat everyone you encounter through the day with the same courtesy and respect you would show a potential customer, then you can't help but be successful in your

> *Excellence is the result of caring more than others think you should, risking more than others think is safe, dreaming more than others think is practical, and expecting more than others think is possible.*

prospecting efforts. Remember that everyone is a potential prospect! Don't prejudge. Make it your daily goal to treat everyone you see as a very important person. Prospecting is a never-ending process, and you never know who will be your next customer.

Cold Calling

Cold calling is the single biggest fear of any salesperson, but if you learn to do it effectively you will actually be dialing for dollars. In my profession as a Realtor, very few of us make cold calls, and very few of us are highly successful. Some full-time Realtors have incomes as low as $12,500 per year. That's pretty sad. But here's my point: Realtors who make a habit of cold calling "For Sale By Owners" (FSBOs) are the ones who are making more money. These homeowners want to sell their house, and you must convince them that you are the one to do it—that is, if you truly believe you can do it. If you are not confident that you're the one, then don't promise something you can't deliver.

I get business because I am so confident. I'm not afraid to tell people that I am the best Realtor to handle their needs. When they look me in the eye, they see someone who is sure of his ability to help them.

Put yourself in the shoes of a potential customer. Would you want to do business with a salesperson who lacks self-confidence? I doubt it. And this is especially true if you're selling an expensive item like a house.

Confidence has a lot to do with success in cold calling. Every salesperson talks about the fear of picking up the phone or knocking on the door of a prospect's home or office. Someone once reminded me that no one ever died from cold calling. That thought stuck with me and made it easier for me to make cold calls. I used to be petrified of cold calling, but not anymore. I don't have a script for you, but I want to give you the confidence to make cold calls. You should make your own script that fits your product or service. Keep it short, sweet, and to the point. Remember that your sole reason for calling is to secure a face-to-face appointment. The best way to learn what techniques work for you is simply to try different approaches and see which ones are most effective.

My advice is to tell your potential customers what you truly believe in your heart about your product or service and how it will benefit them. The difference between features and benefits has been discussed in countless articles, websites, and blogs, but remember that it applies to everything we do. Talk about how your product or service will benefit your customer. When you are cold calling potential customers, you will get the appointment only if they believe that there is something in it for them.

Listen to your heart and let it dictate your words. Enthusiastically describe what your heart is saying. Excitement is contagious, and people like to be around upbeat people. But keep your expectations realistic. Some people may not give you a warm welcome, and a few will even hang up on you. When this happens, just let it go and move on to the next person.

You must schedule your time for cold calling just as you would schedule an appointment. If you don't make time to do it, you will be letting yourself down by limiting what you can achieve. If you are a Realtor, for example, I suggest scheduling cold calls on Tuesday or Thursday night for a two-hour stretch. Don't do anything during that time except make calls and set appointments.

Keep in mind that people want to be sold on you. You may feel a little rusty when you make your first call of the night, but after a while it becomes much easier to talk with prospects. At some point it begins to flow without much effort, and you may feel like you can sell the world. It is so exciting when you set your first appointment of the evening. It will give you a huge rush of adrenaline to keep you going.

Identifying the Decision Maker

There will be times when you call on a company or prospect but you don't know who the decision maker is. Most of us have a hard time getting an opportunity to talk with the right person at a company—the person who has the power to say "yes" or "no" to buying your product or service. Some even call it "getting past the gatekeeper." Often the person who screens calls for a company is the receptionist. You may also deal with an administrative assistant who screens calls for a specific department within the company.

You will hear about many methods of getting past the receptionist or administrative assistant. The one method I have found to be most effective is to be humble and honest. No tricks, just good old-fashioned selling yourself.

Even though the gatekeeper is not the person who will make the decision about buying your product, that doesn't mean you should treat that person with less respect than the potential buyer. If you ask for the gatekeeper's help in reaching the right person and you do it in humble way, your sincerity will come across in your voice and make that person more likely to help you.

If the company you are calling is local and you have difficulty getting the decision maker's name over the phone, try visiting their office. Be sure to set an appointment with the gatekeeper rather than dropping in unannounced. When you stop by, ask the gatekeeper who would be the best person for you to contact.

Remember that if you are humble first, everything else will fall into place.

Asking for Help

Your personal sphere of influence is your main target area for locating potential customers. You will have a better chance of doing business as a result of friendship and networking than through cold calling. Because of the trust that normally exists among friends, you will not have to rely as much on name recognition.

How many people know what you do for a living? Probably not enough. Everyone you know should have a supply of your business cards. Be humble when asking for referrals.

It shouldn't be a secret what you sell. Celebrate it. Tell the world!

Networking through Your Chamber of Commerce

Joining your local Chamber of Commerce will bring many benefits. Not only will you meet prospective clients at Chamber events, but you'll also receive a directory of the major companies in your area, with the name of a contact person for each company. These directories are often included as part of your membership benefits or provided at a discount to Chamber members.

In larger metropolitan areas, the Chamber will have many groups that you can join. If it costs you $400 per year to belong to the Chamber and you get only one good lead, it will have been worth it. I've been a member since I started my business, and it has done a number of positive things for me. The main reason to get involved is for the contacts. The more people you know, the more people you will be able to do business with.

In addition to joining the Chamber of Commerce, join other organizations that will benefit your business. The more networking opportunities you pursue, the better chance you will have of achieving success.

Preparing to Meet with Clients

Before you meet with a prospective customer, do as much research as possible. Be resourceful in finding information. Go to the library, check stock quotes, visit the company's website, and so on. Find out about the prospect's company so you can talk intelligently about their needs when you meet with them for the first time.

It's extremely satisfying to a customer when you go in with your pen and paper and also bring a little "cheat sheet" about the company so you can ask questions. Always take notes when talking with prospective clients—it makes them feel important.

The library and Internet are good places to begin your research, and another excellent way to get information is to talk with someone who is familiar with your prospect's company.

Dealing with Voice Mail

In today's fast-paced world, most of us will not immediately reach the person we're trying to call. Often we will be transferred to that person's voice mail. Always be prepared to leave a message. Jot down several thoughts about what you want to say. You can even create a brief script for voice mail messages.

Be organized when leaving a voice mail message. Don't speak too long. If you keep your message brief, your prospective customer will want to call you back for more information.

Voice mail is an opportune way to let people hear your friendly voice. Remember that this person is probably getting a ton of voice mail. Give them a reason to call you back. Make your message exciting, and don't speak in a monotone.

Be sure to leave an inviting message. For example, instead of saying "This is Jane Doe with ABC Company. I'd like to talk with you about our product. Please call me at 555-9999," it would be better to say, "This is Jane Doe with ABC Company. I have some exciting news to talk with you about. Please call me back at your earliest convenience at my direct line, 555-9999."

Another way to motivate people to call you back is to ask for help. For example, you could say, "This is Jane Doe with ABC Company. We have a couple of questions we need to ask you. Please call me back at 555-9999." Always say something that will prompt the listener to call you back. Be creative. Think of something that reflects your personality.

I recommend leaving the phone number of your direct line and mentioning this in your message. This will impress your prospective customers. Let them know they can reach you at any time. By leaving the number of your direct line and letting prospects know they can reach you after office hours, you are already starting to build a personal relationship. If someone calls you back in the evening and asks if it's a bad time to call, reassure them by saying, "No, I just got done feeding the kids (or putting them to bed). This is a great time to call." You are sharing some personal information—the fact that you have a family—while letting them know that you are looking forward to talking with them. Tailor your response to fit your situation.

Setting Appointments

When you are making cold calls or prospecting over the phone, keep in mind that your sole objective is to set an appointment for a face-to-face meeting. Never lose sight of this! Your purpose is not to sell something over the phone unless you are in telesales.

Remember that people are used to hearing canned presentations on the phone. You must sound natural, warm, and friendly. Pretend the person you are calling is sitting right in front of you. Your voice must convey the same warmth over the phone that it would have if they were in the same room with you.

Keep a mirror within visual range and check your appearance periodically. Are you smiling as you speak? Do you appear poised and professional? If not, you may be sending the wrong message. You may find it helpful to practice with a partner. Choose someone you trust to provide honest feedback about your phone presentation.

Be respectful of the other person's time. I recommend starting out by asking, "Is this a bad time to be calling?" or "Do you have just a few minutes?" Develop an opening that is natural for you. Whatever that opening is, let them know that you respect their time. Nothing is more irritating than to pick up the phone and have someone launch into a long-winded spiel when you are right in the middle of a project or task.

Use a script as your guide when cold calling. Practice this script until it sounds natural. You don't want to make it obvious that you are using a script. Keep the script short and to the point. Avoid any long, drawn-out dialogue. Use language that has impact without being overbearing. One of my favorite things to say during a cold call is "You owe it to yourself to spend 10 minutes with me" or "I'm the one who is going to get you the best deal."

When you set an appointment, offer a choice of several time slots. This keeps you in control. Send a personal note if an appointment is scheduled more than a week in advance. Notes should be written the same time as the conversation, while it is still fresh in your mind. The note should confirm the meeting time, place, and date in addition to conveying your sincere thanks for their time on the phone. Tell them how much you are looking forward to meeting them. A note should also be sent to those who did not book an appointment with you, thanking them for visiting with you on the phone.

Select at least one night or day a week to lock yourself in a room for two hours and do nothing but make cold calls. This is your *opportunity time*. Let your family know you are not to be interrupted during this time.

Set a goal for yourself. For example, my goal was always to set five appointments with owners who were trying to sell their own homes. Don't stop calling until you reach your goal.

Being a good listener during cold calls will help you determine what is and isn't working in your presentation. You'll be able to tell during conversations what has turned someone off. Try to put yourself in the other person's shoes. How would you react if someone called you and used the same script you are using?

There are several schools of thought on overcoming objections and how many objections you need to hear before going on to the next call. You should weigh the amount of time you are willing to spend overcoming objections on one call versus how many other calls you could have made during that time. If you feel the prospect is not open to setting an appointment with you after you have addressed an objection or two, move on to the next prospect. I have found that someone who schedules an appointment under pressure is more likely to cancel the appointment. It is even more likely that they will have someone else call you to cancel so as to avoid being pressured by you to keep their appointment.

MIDLANDS BUSINESS JOURNAL • APRIL 9 - 15, 1999 • 9

Deeb: Careful selection of real estate agent ensures favorable experience for consumer

by Amy O'Loughlin

Purchasing or selling a home is no small feat, and consumers should take careful consideration when seeking out real estate professionals to ensure that the process is a favorable one, according to Van Deeb, owner of Deeb & Associates Real Estate Co.

He said a challenge continues to be getting customers to understand the importance of selecting a real estate agent, not just a real estate company.

"When you buy or sell a house, the real estate company doesn't sell the house," Deeb said. "You're using the individual in real estate for the service. You want someone who is honest and whom you are the most comfortable with. You will be working with this person until the job is complete. I tell people to ask three friends who have used a realtor within the past year about who they used."

Deeb said 98 percent of Deeb & Associates' business comes from referrals.

"It doesn't take a rocket scientist to sell real estate," he said. "Anyone can say 'This is the kitchen and this is the bathroom.' What separates a great realtor from an average realtor is customer service. For example, if I don't return somebody's call within an hour or two, I should not expect him to be happy.

"My philosophy has always been that if you take care of people and don't treat them as a number, they will never forget you. People have specific dentists and doctors they go to. I want to have people consider us their real estate company. The only way you grow is by taking care of your customers. What does a small real estate company have to advertise? A sold sign in a yard. That's it."

Deeb said one customer had her home on the market for six months. When he came to the house, he told the woman the atmosphere didn't seem warm and had her put a number

Deeb ... **"You want someone who is honest and whom you are the most comfortable with. You will be working with this person until the job is complete."**

of personal effects throughout the home.

The house was sold two weeks later at a higher price than the original listing.

"We tell sellers to get their houses ready as if they were going to buy it," Deeb said. "We educate sellers on what they have to do to get their house sold, but we're not going to tell them something just to get the listing. We don't just tell people what they want to hear. You can't just stick a sign in a yard and wait for an offer."

He said because of technological advances, consumers are becoming more knowledgeable about the real estate

industry and the buying and selling processes.

"The biggest way technology has changed the industry is that it used to take two weeks to find out if your loan was approved," Deeb said. "Now it takes about an hour."

He said he has incorporated the use of a digital camera to take pictures of the exteriors and any part of the interiors in homes shown to clients.

"At the end of the tour I give them the disk," Deeb said. "People who are relocating especially like it because chances are the transferee couldn't bring his whole family on the
Continued on next page.

---

10 • APRIL 9 - 15, 1999 • MIDLANDS BUSINESS JOURNAL

Deeb & Associates

Continued from preceding page.

home-buying trip. He could just overnight the disk and the family could view the choices on their home computer."

He said he provides the service for visitors at open houses as well.

Deeb & Associates has worked on a number of relocations for Aquila Energy.

Deeb said the company has had listings in all price ranges and areas of town.

"We will go wherever," he said. "We're very diverse and sell in all parts of Omaha."

Deeb & Associates had $26 million in sales in 1998. Deeb said revenues have increased, at a minimum, 15 to 25 percent each year.

"The market has always been pretty good here," he said.

Deeb started the company in December 1993. He moved the home-based business to 90th and Dodge a year later and then moved to 11712 W. Dodge Road Feb. 10.

Deeb & Associates has 15 agents. A number of them work out of their homes.

Deeb said he would like to have 30 agents by the end of the year and wants to add 10 to 15 agents each year after that.

Envisioning Success

Three key factors in achieving top sales performance are knowing how to set goals, being able to visualize exactly what you want to accomplish, and having the self-discipline to follow through with your plans. If you read this chapter and apply the skills and techniques covered here, you'll be amazed at the improvement in your sales performance.

Goal Setting

A multitude of studies have shown that the most accomplished leaders in every field are the ones who set specific goals. All of the top sales performers I have known could immediately recite their goals when asked. There is no doubt in my mind that it is impossible to be a high achiever without setting goals.

Goals serve several purposes. First, they provide you with a road map that enables you to track your progress and to see when you've made a detour from your goals.

Second, goal setting makes you accountable for your actions on a daily, weekly, monthly, quarterly, and annual basis. When you set clear and understandable goals, you can determine whether your actions are moving you toward or away from them. Goals keep you on track.

Third, goals help you organize your time. For example, let's say you want to add one new customer to your business each week. You know your average is one new customer out of three appointments, and it takes four hours of cold calling to set three appointments. Each appointment takes approximately one hour. You can now schedule the appropriate amount of time you will need to devote to these activities in order to reach your goal of adding one new customer each week.

> *Your goals should be individualized, realistic, measurable, and written.*

To have a positive impact on your sales performance, you must make sure that your goals are individualized, realistic, measurable, and written. I believe goals should also reflect reasonable and above-average levels of accomplishment. In other words, the intention to merely get through the year without being fired only requires minimal performance, does not demonstrate an above-average level of accomplishment, and should not be considered a goal.

Individualized goals are those you personally want to achieve, not goals other people have set for you or duplicates of someone else's goals. This may seem obvious to you, but I make the point because I have seen salespeople strive to achieve the goals of top performers and come up short because these goals didn't have the necessary individualized qualities and therefore lacked motivational appeal.

An example will help to illustrate this point about setting individualized goals. Let's say you have consistently been second in sales in your division and are satisfied with this, yet you are really frustrated that a prime customer continues to elude you. Make the customer your goal instead of trying to be number one in your division.

Realistic goals are those that require some stretching without being out of reach. I have witnessed good salespeople fall short of unrealistic goals and then beat themselves up about it, even though their performance was admirable. By setting unrealistic goals, they have turned a positive outcome (admirable performance) into a negative one (loss of confidence because they didn't meet their goals). If you, for instance, are a junior salesperson servicing one of the weaker territories for your product or service, it may not be realistic for you to attempt to break all sales records. A more productive goal may be to increase the business from established customers by 20 percent and add one new

> *Watch for opportunities and be ready for them whenever they occur.*

customer each week. Tailor your goals to fit your specific situation.

A measurable goal is one that is time-limited and can be numerically defined. Distinguishing between long-term and short-term goals often helps to make them measurable. For example, if my goal is to have 52 residential sales per year, then I know that I will need to have 13 sales by the end of each quarter. I have just broken down my long-term goal into smaller increments or short-term goals. By doing this, I have not only made my goals measurable but also manageable. I can easily track my progress (or lack of it) by comparing my performance in each quarter to my short-term goals. In doing this, I am making myself continuously accountable and less likely to procrastinate.

I can't stress enough the importance of writing down your goals. If you are willing to take the time to set goals, then take the time to commit your goals to writing. All top sales performers write down their goals and review them periodically. This is the only way to track your progress and continuously assess the effectiveness of your work.

I recommend taking several days or even a week in December to focus on setting your goals for the next year. This is your time to reflect on your productivity during the past year and to set up your personal *game plan* for the coming year. I do this each December and look forward to this activity with great anticipation. This should be a very exciting time for you, too. Make this activity your No. 1 priority at the end of the year. I am willing to skip some of the holiday festivities, if necessary, to complete my game plan. It's a real thrill to review all of the possible sales objectives available to me, from number of sales, to net income, to extending sales territory, to adding sales support, to earning peer recognition. For me, goal planning is second only to goal attainment as a highlight of my sales year.

Write down everything you intend to achieve by the end of next year, and then choose at least three of those goals that you feel will motivate you throughout the year. Break those goals into smaller, short-term goals. They can be weekly, monthly, or quarterly, depending on your situation.

Next, create goal posters to map out your strategy for success. You should make one poster for each long-term goal. Each goal poster should be large enough to accommodate all of your short-term goals or stops along the way to your long-term goal. I frequently use a piece of poster board 4 feet wide and 2 feet high and begin by plotting my year-end goal on the right and my monthly or quarterly goals at intervals starting from the left. As I achieve my short-term goals, I mark

> *Let people see what you have in your heart, including aggressiveness, ambition, and passion.*

my progress on the poster board. This serves as a constant reminder that I'm making headway, helping me to stay motivated.

After you have spent time establishing your goals for the coming year, share them with your immediate superior and ask for feedback and advice. When I worked for a homebuilder, I shared my goals with my boss and said, "If there's anything I'm not doing that I should be doing, please tell me. And if there's anything you see me do that you think is preventing me from meeting my goals, please tell me that as well." Then I asked my supervisor what expectations or goals she had in mind for me. This is one of the best ways I know to be accountable and leave your superior with a positive impression of you. If you are self-employed, then share your goals with someone who will directly benefit from the successful achievement of your goals. This may be a spouse or partner who will support your progress and encourage you toward prosperity. Choose someone who has a strong interest in your success.

Here's a quick summary of my suggestions for goal setting:

1. Set aside a special time to set goals and WRITE THEM DOWN!

2. Set goals that are individualized, realistic, measurable, and written.

3. Break down long-term goals into smaller increments or short-term goals.

4. Share your goals with a superior, spouse, or someone who wants you to succeed.

5. Follow your game plan!

Although we have focused primarily on setting professional goals, a well-balanced individual will also establish goals for other aspects of life such as family, social, personal development, and spiritual areas. You may find that meeting your professional goals will allow you to meet some of the goals in other areas of your life. For example, increasing your income may help you meet a social goal such as joining a country club or a personal development goal such as taking night courses to complete a degree or earn professional accreditation. The increased income may also allow you to meet a family goal of taking a relaxing vacation together. You can see how the practice of goal setting not only helps you focus on your professional development but on other aspects of your life as well.

Visualization: The reward picture

Napoleon Hill, the author of *Think and Grow Rich*, wrote, "If you can conceive it and believe it, you can achieve it." This statement has proven to be true in my own life and has remained with me ever since the first time I heard it. I believe in visualizing goals. Decide where you want to be in life and picture yourself at that level.

To drive home the power of visualization, I will share a personal story. In high school I was more interested in being the class clown than in athletics, and although I made the football team, I didn't get much playing time. I considered myself too small to play at the level of my buddies, several of whom were all-state players. I saw myself as unable to compete with the bigger, more talented players.

After graduation I knew that I wanted to play college football, but my confidence was a little shaky, to say the least. I talked with two of my high school coaches. One was quite frank in his appraisal of my ability and tried to discourage me from setting myself up for disappointment. The other offered more encouraging advice. He said, "If you really want it, you'll work hard enough to achieve it." That was the message I had been waiting to hear! I began to see myself as a college athlete.

Of course, I knew visualization alone would not be enough. I began to focus on improving myself physically. During the summer I worked out with weights to increase my muscle mass and ran to build up endurance. To my amazement, my dedication put me in the starting lineup on the junior varsity football team, ahead of some of my all-state counterparts from different high schools.

I continued to keep football as a priority, and I spent many weekend nights lifting weights or running the stadium stairs instead of partying with my buddies.

The connection between visualization, hard work, and achievement was becoming very real for me.

The season finale Red/White game was about a week away. I felt a power and potential within me that gave me the conviction that I could not only play but could stand out and do something exceptional. Specifically, I envisioned myself intercepting a pass and scoring a touchdown!

During the week before the game, I followed a nightly ritual that strengthened this vision. While washing my face before bed, I would splash water on my face six times and then look in the mirror and yell "TOUCHDOWN!" while raising both arms in the air to signify an official touchdown. To further strengthen this vision, I told my friends I was going to pick off a pass and score.

Can you guess what happened? The game was played in a driving rain, and conditions were difficult. The score was 7–7 at the beginning of the second quarter. With minutes left in the second half, I intercepted a pass from our first-string quarterback (who later made it to the final cut with the Dallas Cowboys), then ran 32 yards as fast as I could to the end zone.

TOUCHDOWN! My team won 13–7 with my six points! My friends listening to the game on the radio couldn't believe it—not only that it had happened, but also that I had predicted it would happen. I had visualized it, I wanted it, and it happened.

This was my first concrete experience with visualization, and it made me a confirmed believer in the principle that whatever we can perceive and believe, we can achieve—if we take the necessary actions to make it happen.

I was able to accomplish something unique and valuable because I visualized not only the outcome but also the activity it would take to reach that outcome.

> *One of the many functions of a leader is to look into the future and see the organization not as it is, but as it can be one day.*

Visualization is not just critical to the success of the high achiever, it's mandatory for everyone who wants to get somewhere in life. If we don't know where we want to go, we're just wandering, and we may not get anywhere. When our goals are not visualized, they are merely fantasies or daydreams.

Visualization means watching something happen in your own mind and feeling the emotions attached to it. You should be animated when talking about your vision, and others should get excited hearing you explain it.

When you think about it, the need for visualization is painfully obvious. How can we say we want to have or be something if we can't visualize it? Intensifying the visualization by attaching emotions to it is just a natural extension that promotes stronger motivation. When we are highly motivated, we will work harder. Everyone who desires high achievement must visualize a reward picture, feel the enjoyment of the picture, look back from the picture to appreciate the effort it takes to get there, and follow through on that effort.

Visualization never worked better for me than it did with my first real estate job. I was 22 years old and had moved from Omaha to Dallas. While working as a waiter, I became friends with a banker who suggested I get into real estate. Home sales were rising in 1983 in Dallas and it would be, he suggested, a great opportunity for someone with my ambition.

Since a real estate license was not required to work as a salesperson for a homebuilder, I immediately began to call homebuilders. Pulte, one of the biggest homebuilders in Dallas, said their policy was for applicants to send in a job application or résumé. I was too excited to wait for the completion of that process, so I went straight to Pulte's office and asked to see one of their sales managers (Pulte had several). The receptionist told me that only one sales manager was available but that I couldn't see her without an appointment. I said I'd wait, and wait I did. After several hours the sales manager came out of her office to see this young man who wouldn't go away. I handed her the résumé I had prepared, and then I started talking as quickly and convincingly as I could.

My résumé was devoid of sales experience except for being crowned "King of the Carnival" in second grade for selling the most raffle tickets. The sales manager was good-natured and amused by my manic presentation, and she asked me why I thought I could sell homes. "If I'm not your top salesman in three months," I told her, "you won't have to fire me because I will resign." I'd never sold a fence post, let alone real estate, but I had confidence in my potential for success!

The sales manager was far from convinced but instructed me to be a "host" for an open house. Whenever Pulte was going to hire a new salesperson, they would have that individual go to a model home, sit with two salespeople, and greet potential buyers as they entered the house and try to determine their level of interest before they were approached by an actual salesperson. The salespeople showing the house that day reported to the sales manager that I was assertive and friendly. They recommended hiring me. I completed a condensed training program and covered the regular two-week program in two days! I learned how to figure mortgages, complete sales contracts, qualify buyers, and so on.

Every quarter, the Pulte divisions had a formal banquet where prizes were announced and the prestigious President's Award—the cream of the crop—was presented. This quarterly awards banquet was a major event for Pulte Homes and was always held in one of the most elegant hotels in Dallas. It would be my first black-tie occasion at my first real job.

Before I had even sold one home, I began practicing my acceptance speech for the President's Award. I rehearsed in my car while driving between appointments. I saw myself as the winner. I felt the admiration and amazement of my peers. I heard the applause after my speech and witnessed the pride on my sales manager's face. I lived that experience over and over again. Several times I got so engrossed that I missed my exit while I was driving.

> *"If you can dream it, you can do it."*
>
> *Walt Disney*

During my first three months at Pulte Homes I worked seven days a week and used every chance I had to meet new people and make sure they knew that I was selling homes. I arrived at open houses early and stayed late. I wanted to live that reward picture in real life so badly that I focused 100 percent of my energy on creating an opportunity whenever I was around people in any situation. The biggest challenge for me was that I was still new to the Dallas area and had very few contacts and practically no network. I didn't see that as an obstacle but as an opportunity to create a network. During that three-month period, I sold 40 homes.

Although I was confident of a top prize at the banquet, I didn't know my place for sure because there were more than 50 salespeople in the company and no one knew the sales volumes of the others. My heart was pounding when my sales manager took the stage. As she started talking, I began to live my reward picture. "Before I present the President's Award," she told the crowd, "I want to tell you a story about the recipient." She then related my brash prediction about being the top salesperson at my first interview.

I'd like to tell you that I ran up to the stage and confidently gave the speech that I had envisioned a thousand times. The truth is that I was so emotional that I couldn't remember a word of it! However, everything else about the evening was just as I had pictured it. The applause, the congratulations, the amazement because I was new to Dallas all happened as I had imagined. It was the most exciting event of my life except for the birth of my daughter, Courtney, a few years later. As important as the reward itself was for me, even more profound was the knowledge that I could use visualization to achieve whatever I wanted in my career.

Visualization is second nature to me now, and it has never failed me. Whenever I get the opportunity, I tell others about the power of visualization for developing intrinsic motivation. Every accomplishment of mine was born from the vision or reward picture of that accomplishment.

Visualization and motivation go hand in hand. To strengthen motivation toward a goal, make the reward picture as real as possible and reinforce it daily. See yourself receiving the award, feel the excitement and pride that goes with it. Create a detailed vision of you achieving your goal! Who is presenting it to you? Visualize the person handing you the award, hear the applause of the audience, see the admiration on the faces of your peers. Carry a visible reminder of your goal with you always.

During the last quarter of 1991, a close Realtor friend of mine had won a plaque that identified him as one of the top 20 real estate producers in Texas. Seeing his plaque gave me an intense desire to win one myself for the first quarter of 1992. I knew visualization would be the key. I took a snapshot of his plaque, mounted it on an 8-1/2 by 11 inch sheet of red paper, had it laminated, punched a hole in one corner and attached it to my keychain. I also wrote on it in big letters, "I will have one of these on my wall for the first quarter of 1992."

Attaching my goal to my keychain meant that everybody could see it. When I was driving my car, that 8-1/2 by 11 laminated sheet of paper would be dangling from the keychain. Whenever anyone got in my car—customers who were looking at houses, friends, anyone else—everybody would comment on it: "Van, what is that hanging from your keychain?" So what did I get a chance to do? I got a chance to talk about my goal. I told them all about it, and what did they want to do? They wanted to help me. They wanted to refer me to people who were interested in buying or selling a house, because I carried around a visual reminder of my goal.

The same thing happened whenever I went into a restaurant. Where do you put your keychain when you go into a restaurant? You put it in your pocket. Well, I couldn't put an 8-1/2 by 11 laminated sheet of paper in my pocket, so I would lay it on the table. Not only would I be asked about it by the person with whom I was sharing a meal, but even the servers would ask me what it was. Once again, I had a chance to talk about my goal of being one of the top 20 real estate producers in Dallas.

Everywhere I went, I took my keys with me. It was obvious that there was something attached to my keychain, and people would inquire about it. What a great opportunity for me to tell them what that sheet of paper meant to me. It got the attention of everyone I came into contact with, and I got a chance to talk about my goals and ask them to help me: "Gosh, I would love to not have this on my keychain next year, so if you happen to know anyone who wants to buy or sell a house, I sure would appreciate it if you would give them my name and phone number so I can accomplish my goal."

This was a goal visualization technique that served as a constant visual reminder of my goal. Everyone I came in contact with asked me about it, and I verbally reinforced my vision each time I responded to an inquiry. Sharing my goal with so many other people made me feel accountable to follow through and win the plaque. The visual and verbal cues kept me strongly focused on my goal. As a result, I was the third highest producer for the first quarter of 1992 and received my plaque! The gratification of receiving the award and the recognition was so intense that I can still feel it as I write about it.

Taking action on your vision or reward picture will make a measurable difference in your level of accomplishment, whether your goal is to be top dog or just to add one new customer account each month. Visualizing the accomplishment, big or small, is the first step toward achievement.

Here are some practical steps to get you started:

- Put your goal on every mirror in your house, on your refrigerator, on your bedroom and bathroom doors, on your car dashboard, and on your desk.

- Create an internal sense of excitement each time you view or talk about the goal.

- Attend award functions to get an appreciation of the winners' feelings.

- Write affirmations of your goal and say them out loud to yourself daily.

- Create visual representations of the effects of your achievement. For example, you could carry around a picture of the new car you plan to buy with your additional income or a travel brochure of the trip you plan to take once you've achieved your goal.

- Tell supportive others about your goal.

Visualize

By Natalie J.S. Hadley

Deeb spells out importance of community contributions

At a recent Greater Omaha Chamber of Commerce event, President David Brown introduced Van Deeb as a philanthropist.

In response, the president of Deeb Realty quipped, "I've never been introduced as something I couldn't spell."

Deeb described himself as something a little easier to spell: a visualist.

"Everything we've accomplished as a company, I have visualized before we got there," he said of the 115-agent residential real estate company he started 11 years ago in his garage. "I visualize our company doing great things for this city."

Deeb's community contributions so far have focused on youth, particularly athletics. For 10 years, he brought attention to Children's Hospital with his annual stint on the building's roof, where he stayed until donors had contributed $10,000. He retired from roof sitting two years ago.

"I'm actually afraid of heights," he said, laughing. "Now I'm using my energy in other areas."

Deeb Realty sponsors the American Legion baseball team at Burke High School where Deeb's only child, Courtney, is a freshman and where Deeb himself was recently inducted into the hall of fame for his years playing football. The company also sponsors baseball, football, basketball and volleyball at Millard North High School, the city of Bellevue's summer youth programs, and athletic programs at the University of Nebraska at Omaha, where Deeb played football from 1977 to 1981.

"It's expensive for parents today to have their kids play sports," Deeb said. "Turning to corporate sponsors eliminates the need for car wash fundraisers every day."

Raising Courtney alone gave Deeb an appreciation for the challenges some parents face. "My daughter was born on my birthday, August 24, so that was special," he said. "Here I had this healthy baby, but I knew several people who had babies around the same time who weren't as fortunate. I wanted to help, so I started raising money for Children's Hospital."

Deeb plans to expand his personal and corporate philanthropy to include Omaha firefighters, law enforcement and teachers.

"Someday I'd like to sponsor teacher, firefighter and law enforcement officer of the year awards," said Deeb.

"It's expensive for parents today to have their kids play sports... Turning to corporate sponsors eliminates the need for car wash fundraisers every day."

Van Deeb

continued on next page

Deeb in his office... "If you have drive, desire and determination, there's nothing you can't do."

continued from previous page

The youngest of five children, Deeb described himself as a "ham" who got a taste of sales early on.

"I knew I wanted to be in sales when I sold the most carnival tickets in second grade at Mount View Elementary," he said. "As an adult, I found out real estate is one of the biggest tickets you can sell."

After 12 years in the real estate business, Deeb decided to open his own company in 1993 because of what he saw as limitations on the way agents could promote themselves. The company grew to include other agents drawn by a generous commission schedule, superior training and no monthly fees, Deeb said.

"Almost 90 percent of real estate agents get out of the business in their first two years," he said. "Ours don't because there are no fees, they are continuously trained, and they make what they are worth."

The formula appears to be working. Deeb Realty made number 19 on the Greater Omaha Chamber of Commerce's list of the city's 25 fastest growing companies, based on revenue of the past three years. This is the first year Deeb Realty has made the list, and it is the only real estate firm this time.

Another sign of growth came in the purchase of a new building at 117th and West Center Road in mid-March. The new building has 7,500 square feet, compared with 1,000 at the previous location, giving the company room to add 200 more peo-

ple. The company also made the decision to shorten its name from Deeb and Associates Real Estate Company to Deeb Realty.

"Our goal is to be the best real estate firm in Omaha," Deeb said. "We also plan to open offices in Council Bluffs and Lincoln within the next two years."

Deeb still sells real estate himself, mostly for family and friends, but devotes most of his time to managing the company and training agents. In 1996 he wrote a book called "Selling From the Heart" that he gives away at speaking engagements.

"I do motivational speaking as a hobby," he said. "I get a thrill out of seeing an average salesman become great. If you have drive, desire and determination, there's nothing you can't do."

Those qualities and a stubborn streak propelled Deeb when he started his company.

"I had the owners of two of the larger firms in town say there wasn't room for another real estate company," he said. "If someone says, 'Van, you can't,' I'll say, 'Watch me.'"

Deeb said he believes self motivation can be taught.

"Everyone has greatness inside," he said. "Sometimes it takes a little push to bring it out. I've lived my whole life off motivation – and my parents' homemade cooking."

He laughed. "I bought a building four blocks from their house, so I can eat lunch there every day." mᵐm

For further help in establishing goals that are realistic for you, re-read the section on goal setting at the beginning of this chapter.

A few years ago I watched a Barbara Walters interview with Jim Carrey, an actor who has starred in several movies. Carrey told a story about how he used visualization to reach a goal. In December of 1990, Carrey wrote a check to himself for $10 million. At that time he was living out of his vehicle, basically broke. He carried the check around in his wallet and made a promise to himself that by November of 1995 he would receive a check for $10 million. Just before Thanksgiving in 1995, Carrey started making $10 million for each movie he did. That, my friends, is the power of visualization.

Starting the Day

I firmly believe that the early bird *does* get the worm. My most productive days are those that start at 4:30 a.m. I grab my workout clothes that I've laid out the night before and head to my health club. I get a great workout or sometimes opt for the "executive workout," which involves sitting in the steam room and taking a lot of time to get ready.

You'll find that a health club membership will pay for itself many times over. You'll be up with the other motivated early-risers and have a chance to network with serious business people. By 7:00 at the latest, I've greeted nearly everyone I see, introducing myself to people I haven't met before. Look at all the networking I've done, and the sun has barely had a chance to rise. This is a great way to start your day. Working out in the morning always energizes me for the day ahead.

Every morning I give myself a pep talk. This might sound strange, but it works—at least, it works for me. I tell myself things like "Don't come home until you've been productive" or "Nobody is responsible for the outcome of today except me." I get myself as fired up as I possibly can, so I am prepared and ready for my first customer.

I realize that going to a health club early in the day is not for everyone. Taking kids to school or preparing the family breakfast may mean that my routine is impossible for you. However, *find a way* to spend a little time with yourself before you start your work day, even if it means giving yourself a pep talk in the car as you are driving to work.

One of the companies I worked for in the past started every sales meeting by playing a cassette tape of the theme from "Rocky." I thought that was great, and man, did it pump me up. I felt like decking the salesman next to me after hearing that! Seriously, this kind of stuff really works.

I never could tolerate caffeine until later in life, so I was not much of a morning coffee drinker. My energy came naturally. (Today I can't wait for my first cup!)

How you start the day depends a lot on how you have prepared yourself the night before. I make a to-do list of all the things I want to accomplish the next day, and then I prioritize the items in order of importance.

> *The difference between an unsuccessful salesperson and a successful one is not a lack of ability or a lack of knowledge, but a lack of will.*

Try to schedule your less appealing tasks early in the day. Get the negatives out of the way first, such as telling a customer bad news or returning a call from an angry or upset customer. If you don't take care of these things right away in the morning, they will be on your mind all day, sapping your energy and reducing your productivity.

Accepting Advice

"He who scorns instruction will pay for it, but he who respects a command is rewarded." (Proverbs 13:13)

This is one of my favorite proverbs because it contains so much wisdom. If someone is giving you instruction, motivation, constructive criticism, or any type of direction, they are probably doing it because they care about you. Be thankful if you are lucky enough to have someone in your life who cares so much about you that they are willing to take their valuable time to help you.

Listening to advice and taking it to heart can help you live a better life, help you become a better business person, help you become more spiritual. It can help you become a better son, daughter, father, mother, brother, or sister.

I don't believe a proverb is considered a "command" but more as a form of encouragement. This proverb encourages us to look for direction from others as to how to be a better employee, business owner, manager, community leader, and so on.

The benefits of accepting advice can be applied to all aspects of our lives. I can't say it enough: be thankful if someone cares about you enough to want only good things to happen to you.

How you choose to deliver advice or instruction to others is another matter. I won't give you too much advice on how to do that, because I have been told I am way too direct when I give instruction or discipline. Fortunately people know I am sincere and that I care deeply about the person I am talking to.

We all need people who care enough about us to be willing to offer help even when we don't ask for it.

Do You Qualify for Your Own Goals?

Everyone tells you to set goals, and I assume you are doing that. The question I'd like to ask you is "Do you qualify for your own goals?"

Are you talking the talk and walking the walk? It is very easy to grab a sheet of paper and begin writing down your goals—where you want to be by the end of this quarter or the end of the year. Maybe you have broken them down to daily, weekly, and monthly goals as I recommended earlier in this chapter.

Writing down your goals is not enough, however. Are you doing anything to make sure you are not just wasting time and the ink and sheet of paper you are writing them on?

Ask yourself these questions:

1. Am I committed to accomplishing these goals?

2. Am I taking the necessary steps to achieve the results I wrote down?

3. Do I need to change my lifestyle to make things happen?

4. Am I willing to make the necessary changes in my daily routine?

5. Have I told my supporters, family, loved ones, manager, or employees about my goals?

6. Have I displayed these goals in places that are visible to remind me of them every day?

Many people say they have goals, but for too many their goals are just words on a piece of paper. In order to qualify for your own goals you have to ask yourself the questions above. You will probably need to make some changes in your life. If no changes were necessary, you would have been accomplishing your goals all the time and it would have become routine. The nice thing about goals is that it is never too late to set them and start pursuing them.

When I suggest making changes I am referring to maybe going to bed an hour earlier in the evening, watching TV an hour less each day, or getting up an hour earlier in the morning. You might need to drink less alcohol to keep your mind sharp, maybe quit smoking and eat less. Maybe you are in a relationship that is keeping you from spending time on your goals. Focus on changing whatever YOU feel could be holding you back from qualifying for your own goals.

Even the slightest bit of change in any of these areas may help you accomplish your goals. One of my favorite ways to achieve a goal I have set for myself is to try to find a way to make it fun. We all love fun in any capacity. If we think something is fun, then we are usually going to see it through. I have found that being successful is fun and rewarding, to say the least.

Re-read the section on visualization and see how I made it fun to accomplish a sales goal.

I am asking you the question, "Do you qualify for your own goals?" because you are the only one who can truly answer it. It's like building a home—it won't

> *Persistence is the fuel that allows ordinary people to attain extraordinary results.*

stand long if it's not on a solid foundation. Your foundation is making sure that you are justifying the path you will take and the changes you will have to make to see that your goals become a reality.

Take setting goals seriously, make changes in your life, make it fun, and you will see results... period.

You Get What You Work For

We have all heard people say that "you get what you pay for." I believe that is true, but I also believe that in the business world you get what you work for. If you are lucky enough to have passion for your career, then work will not seem quite as much like work.

There is no replacement for hard work or working smart in your career. With this attitude and a good solid work ethic you can usually control your own destiny.

I view hard work as the flight path to my desired destination. W-O-R-K, that four-letter word, will help you accomplish all your dreams and goals. Over time you will realize what will benefit you and what is a waste of time, but the only way to find out if something works for you is to try it. How do you know if your efforts will bear fruit if you aren't willing to try new things? What works very well for some people may not have the same results for you, and what works for you may not work for someone else.

The race to be the best in your industry has no finish line.

Without putting forth enough effort to achieve a challenging goal, you will never know what your full potential is.

One of my biggest assets is the capacity and motivation to work hard for something that I want to accomplish. However, after all my years in sales I am still trying to figure out how to work smarter. This is a never-ending challenge, but as long as I am working hard on something, I know I will eventually come up with smarter ways to get the same results without putting in so much time and effort.

When you are a top salesman or a leader in any industry you will always have people gunning for you and even trying to create obstacles to make it more difficult for you to get where you want to go. If you incorporate an unstoppable work ethic, then your competitors will have a hard time doing just that—stopping you.

God gave us many abilities, and the capacity to work hard and long is one of them. You need to be willing to devote lots of time to getting your work done.

People used to roll their eyes when I told them that sometimes I would start my day at 4 a.m. just to get a jump on the world, but it paid off. Today I have no regrets for the long hours I put into building my career.

If you give yourself a task or your boss assigns a project to you, don't put forth only the minimum amount of effort. Do more than what is required, work hard on it, go above and beyond the call of duty. What a great way to stand out within your company—

to be known as the hardest worker in the firm. And what comes with that title are usually big rewards and dividends.

If you ever become self-employed like I did in my early twenties, the work ethic you have established in your job will help you achieve success after you become your own boss.

You could say I didn't outsmart anybody; instead, I outworked them. If you really think about it, though, outworking someone is the same as outsmarting them, because apparently they aren't smart enough to work hard!

Want to be the best at what you do? Then WORK at it. Yes, it's that simple!

True leaders have the confidence to stand alone, the courage to make tough decisions, and the compassion to listen to the needs of others. They prove their leadership by example, by their actions, by their passion and their ability to convince others that we all are created equal and have the same God-given opportunity to accomplish whatever goals or results we are hoping to achieve during our very short time on this earth.

Follow-up Strategies

Attracting new customers is essential for success in sales, but retaining your past customers is just as important. The best way to do this is to stay in touch and provide a consistently high level of customer service. Your goal should be to surprise and delight your existing customers by providing such exceptional service that they will be eager to refer people to you.

PhD in Customer Service
Once you've mastered the art of customer service, you've mastered the art of sales and your business will go through the roof.

I believe you can sell anything to anybody if you love what you are selling. If we can teach people to back into the sale by starting out with customer service, we will have accomplished a great deal. For example, when you make a sales call on someone who is unfamiliar with you or your product and you are up against several competitors, be sure to ask a number of questions. If you take notes on what they tell you, your prospective customers will be impressed that you are making an effort to understand their needs and preferences. If you are competing with several other companies in the same industry, customer service is what will set you apart.

Be flexible! I know a successful business executive who holds appointments while he's at his health club working out on the treadmill. Offer to meet at any location that is convenient for your customer. Ask "Is there any activity you may be doing where we could talk while you're doing it?" Go out of your way to show respect for your prospective customer's time limitations and busy schedule. This is especially important when you are trying to get your foot in the door.

> *If you don't take good care of your customers... somebody else will.*

A major aspect of customer service is making yourself as accessible as possible to your customers. This means that in addition to having an assistant, you give people your direct phone number. You want to be known as someone who returns calls promptly, and carrying a cell phone allows you to provide better follow-up and make efficient use of your time. When your customers have questions or problems, don't leave them waiting to hear from you. Treat each customer as a VIP and you'll earn their loyalty.

Holiday Cards to Everyone

I believe in sending out cards for all kinds of occasions: Christmas, Easter, birthdays—you get the point. Make sure your Christmas cards don't say "Merry Christmas," because some of the recipients may not be Christian. You are always safe with "Happy Holidays" or one of my favorites, "Peace on Earth."

Don't skimp on the cost when it's time to buy holiday cards. The nicer it is, the more it will be remembered. I strongly recommend sending a card with a picture of you and your family on it. Send as many as you can. Send them to prospects, past clients, friends, and family members. Mail cards to city officials (including the mayor) and CEOs of companies. I did this for years, and when I went into a customer's home in July I would often see my card on their refrigerator.

I also recommend sending out holiday cards to all the news anchors and other media figures in your community. Let's say you're taking a customer to lunch and you spot one of your local TV anchors dining at another table. That person is going to remember you from your picture, giving you a legitimate reason to say hello.

It's best to send your holiday cards early in December so people will have time to send one back to you. Many of your past customers will send a card to you in return, and new customers who visit your office will see all the cards you've received. It shows instant acceptance, and your customers will definitely make the connection. Everyone wants to be associated with a well-connected individual.

Sending out holiday cards with your picture is a great way to open doors and build relationships. I can't tell you how many times I've been stopped in malls, grocery stores, and restaurants by strangers who came up to me and said, "Thank you for your nice Christmas card" or "Gee, you have a beautiful daughter!"

If you send a stranger a flyer or marketing piece, their reaction may be, "Gosh, I wish they'd get me off their mailing list." But if you send someone a beautiful holiday card with a picture of your family on it, it will be viewed differently from the impersonal card your competitor will send. Most people are afraid to cross the line between business and personal, but you need to be willing to cross that line. People want to do business with people with whom they feel comfortable, and it helps if they know what you look like.

Business Through Giving

I strongly believe that if you have the ability to do something nice for somebody, you should go ahead and do it. You will never regret it.

A few years ago God blessed me with the ability to help some local families while bringing positive recognition to my company. I was home one night watching the news when a TV reporter talked about a Little League baseball team with around 300 players whose parents had paid a photographer $4,500 to take individual photos and team pictures. The photographer had collected the money upfront without providing the pictures, so the Little League was out all that money. The next day I emailed the reporter and told her I wanted to help out, so she connected me with the Little League president. The reporter thought maybe I would provide a couple of hundred dollars or so, but I told her that I wanted to give the team a check for the entire amount of what they lost. The result was a big news story that was broadcast by radio stations and published in the local newspaper.

When I met the league president the next day at the ballpark to present the check, several parents were on hand to thank me. The looks on their faces showed a deep sense of appreciation. There must have been at least 20 people present on short notice to thank me, and their reaction was truly overwhelming to me. I thank God I had the ability to do that for them.

I felt it in my heart to help these Little League families, and I did. It was as simple as that. How did this act of giving affect my business? More than we will ever be able to measure. Our agents at DEEB Realty benefited greatly because the parents of the baseball players went around bragging about what we did and trying to refer our company whenever possible.

The Little League president called me for two years in a row to invite me to throw out the first pitch of the season and be recognized, and both times I declined because I felt I had received more than enough attention for helping out.

THURSDAY, JULY 19, 2007 **3B**

Donation solves baseball league's photo problems

■ **Many other youth leagues are still waiting for a resolution.**

By **Maggie Creamer**
WORLD-HERALD STAFF WRITER

Van Deeb said he is too old to remember whether he ever played in the Benson Little League. But he does remember attending Mountview Elementary School in Benson and playing sports with his friends every day after school.

So when he found out that the Little League team had not received its individual and team photos from Wurgler Photo, he wanted to help.

"If you have the ability to do something, you should just do it and not waste time talking about it," Deeb said.

Deeb wrote a $4,500 check from Deeb Realty for the Benson Little League to retake individual and team photos. The photos will be retaken at a picnic Saturday.

Wurgler Photo owner Gerald Wurgler took photos for multiple leagues throughout the area in late spring. Many of the parents' checks for those orders were cashed, and they still do not have their photos.

Wurgler, when contacted last month by a reporter, said he had to move out of his office and lost some of his equipment because of financial problems. But he said he was in the process of setting up the remaining equipment and intended to complete the jobs. However, he has not returned repeated phone calls since June 30.

Benson League President Wyatt Gardner said the league planned to dip into its field maintenance funds to pay for the pictures to be retaken and printed.

Gardner said he is relieved the league will not have a financial burden from the photos' expense. If any money is left over, he said, the league will use it to make planned field improvements, including new fencing and bases.

Deeb

Many other leagues, including the Keystone Little League, the Blair Youth Softball Association and teams in the Papillion Recreation Organization, are still waiting and trying to get their photos from Wurgler.

The Omaha Mustangs Midget Football League has not received the photos Wurgler took in December, said freshman cheerleading coach Vickie Beams.

The league has 27 cheerleaders and about 65 football players ages 8 through 14. She said the league plans to have parents file individual complaints with police.

Gardner said he will still try to locate Wurgler and get the photo CDs from him because "there are so many other leagues out there without photos."

Fundraising provides your company with public recognition while giving you a chance to serve your community. I don't believe you should help a group just to get your name on their list of sponsors—pick a group that you believe can do the most to help your community. For example, I support Children's Miracle Network. Several years ago I got the idea to sit on a roof and refuse to come down until I had raised $5,000 for the Children's Miracle Network telethon. Sitting on a roof is an unusual approach to fundraising that brought many positive outcomes. First, it made people aware of the good work that Children's Hospital was doing. Second, I assisted in raising money that helped the kids. Other benefits included presenting a check on TV to a representative of Children's Hospital. Not only did people see me on TV, but they noticed that the check was from my company and they began to associate the event with my company.

Who wouldn't want to do business with someone who has a big heart and raises money for kids? Fundraising also gets you involved in your community. When you do charity work, don't keep it a secret. Go to the media, make public service announcements, and be sure the word gets out about what you are doing. Maybe your story will be unique, like mine. When a guy raises $5,000 by sitting on a roof, it brings name recognition. As with the Christmas cards, when I was out in public people would recognize me and say, "You're the guy who sits on the roof for Children's Hospital." That's a nice association. It tells people that I am involved in my community and that I care about the people in it. Most people will give me a chance to do business with them because they know I'm involved.

If I told you I sat on the roof only to benefit the children, I would not be entirely honest. I did it because I knew I was capable of raising money and it would help make people aware of Children's Hospital. I also did it because it was an excellent way to promote my business. If I can do two things at once, that's great. It's a win-win situation in which everybody benefits.

Stormy weather doesn't stop Deeb from raising money for the Children's Miracle Network

Once again Van C. Deeb, owner of Deeb Real Estate, sat on the rooftop, this year at Grandmother's Restaurant on 90th & Dodge in mid-May to raise money for the Children's Miracle Network Broadcast and Children's Hospital. Deeb was rooftop at 5 a.m. along with Lite 96's Jack and Fred who broadcast their morning show from Grandmother's. Deeb's goal was to raise $10,000 no matter how long he had to stay on the roof. Unfortunately, dangerous lighting and tornado sirens brought Deeb down off the roof shortly after 9 a.m.

"Over $5,000 was raised for the Children's Miracle Network by 9 a.m. which I'm very pleased with," Deeb said.

One hundred percent of all funds raised from the event went to benefit the heartland children served by Children's Hospital. When asked what Deeb's motive was for this unusual event he said, "When I became a father I realized how lucky I was because my daughter was healthy. I know many couples who aren't so lucky. I wanted to give something back … It's that simple.

"I also do this as a local businessman. If I can come up with an idea like sitting on a roof to raise money, anyone can. It is also a way to make people aware that there are so many charities out there that need the communities help."

Deeb went on to thank Rick Windrum, general manager of Grandmother's and said, "Rick was the man behind the scenes and really deserves most of the credit for making the event a success." Two others that have meant a great deal to Deeb are Sally Kahre and Jane Phillips from Children's Hospital. Deeb co-chaired this years CMN Telethon.

Since 1988, over $2.6 million has been raised through the Children's Miracle Network Broadcast to benefit children treated at Children's Hospital. These local funds have helped provide lifesaving medical equipment and additional children's medical services. Children's Hospital is a non-profit organization caring for children since 1948 and the only hospital specifically focused on children in Nebraska. Patients are referred to the 100-bed hospital throughout the region for the treatment of complex or unusual diseases in addition to regular pediatric care.

Children's Hospital is currently constructing a new 225,000 square foot health care facility at 8300 Dodge, across the street from the present hospital, to be completed in the year 2000. Children's has continued to advance as the region's pediatric healthcare provider with nearly 50 percent of its patients now coming from outside the greater metropolitan Omaha area. Many of these children come for specialty clinic visits and outpatient surgeries. At Children's Hospital, no child is turned away due to inability to pay.

For more information on CMN call: 354-7140.

UNITED STATES SENATOR
CHUCK HAGEL
NEBRASKA

May 19, 1999

Mr. Van C. Deeb
Deeb Real Estate
406 N. 90th Street
Omaha, NE 68114

Dear Van:

Thank you for your efforts to raise $10,000 for the
Children's Miracle Network Broadcast.

Your desire to help the heartland children served
by Children's Hospital is inspiring. We're all
grateful for your generosity and creativity.

May the sun shine upon your rooftop. Best wishes
and much continued success.

Regards,

PAID FOR AND AUTHORIZED BY HAGEL FOR NEBRASKA
NOT PRINTED AT GOVERNMENT EXPENSE

Another fundraising idea is to donate to community
or sporting events. For example, I used to donate $10
to Children's Hospital for every 3-point basket a local
basketball team made. This may be too great a financial
commitment for some, but it may not be for others.
Not only does it benefit the children, but it also brings

attention to my business because my contribution is announced on the public address system at every game. Be sure to send press releases to the media when your fundraising efforts are newsworthy.

There are many ways to promote your business while helping your community. Your goal is to meet more people and get your name out so that people think of you in a positive way. Even if you are not able to donate large sums of money, there are countless ways to help others if you feel it in your heart to do so. The cool thing is that it is contagious. Acts of kindness will encourage others to do the same thing.

Most salespeople thrive on recognition because it enhances their business. The more recognition you receive, the more people will want to business with you. Think of as many fundraising ideas as you can. Have fun, and be creative!

Never Assume Anything

One of the biggest downfalls of salespeople is to make assumptions. Never assume something has been done. Always ask and make sure. It's better to follow up than to take a chance that the work is not done the way you want it. A situation arose in our company that illustrated this point.

Our company had a real estate listing but another real estate agency was able to make the sale. When we offer a property for sale, our company always contacts the agent for the buyer to find out which lending company the buyer is going through to obtain their mortgage. In this case the Realtor told us that the buyer was going through a particular mortgage company. That was all the information we needed. It was not our company's job to follow up on the buyer in this situation since he was not our customer. We were representing the seller.

About a week later we called the Realtor again and he couldn't tell us much more than before. I felt he wasn't doing enough follow-up, so I called the mortgage company myself and found out that the buyer hadn't even made the loan application. Frustrated at having to explain to my customers what was holding up the sale of their house, I called this other Realtor and asked, "What's going on?" It seemed that every other word in his explanation was "assumed": "I just assumed that my customer made a loan application"... "I assumed this" and "I assumed that." I had to tell a person who had been in sales twice as long as I had that you should never assume anything. As a result of this Realtor's unfounded assumptions, closings were delayed and people were put in uncomfortable situations.

If you ask your peers or other salespeople if they have ever assumed anything on a sale and been hurt by it in some way, nine out of ten will be able to tell you about a negative outcome that came from making an assumption and failing to follow up. Never assume anything!

When Was the Last Time. . .

When was the last time you invited customers to your office to see your work environment? Not a lot of salespeople do that, and I know many customers who appreciate being invited. Not many of them will take you up on your invitation, but remember that you are trying to build a relationship with your customers, not just make a one-time sale. Invite your customer over for coffee. Be creative; you'll think of something!

When was the last time you bought another industry's trade magazine and looked through it to find ideas that you could adapt to your own business? Most salespeople get their motivation and training solely from their own industry's sales literature and trade magazines. You may be pleasantly surprised at the ideas you can get from industries other than your own.

When was the last time you went to a motivational seminar or sales training session? Even if you are a Top Producer and you think you know all the secrets of selling, you should still go occasionally. I have always said that even if you are sitting there thinking "I know this, and I know that" about everything the speaker says, it is still worth your time if you gain even one new idea or bit of information. It could make the difference in getting a sale.

I have found that most seminars are worth attending because I learn something new and valuable each time. Make time to go, because it is good for business and it keeps you motivated.

All the Right Tools

Being careful about your appearance is important because it shows respect for your customers. Always wear nice business clothes to a sales call—polished shoes and so on. You know what I'm talking about, so I don't need to go into detail.

Be accessible! When your customers call you, it's because they want to talk to you *today*. This goes back to customer service. I recommend giving your direct phone number to your customers, but if you choose not to do this, make sure your assistant phones you immediately if someone calls you. Check your voice mail several times throughout the day.

Don't leave a pager number. Think about the convenience of your customer. Let's say you have a pager and someone pages you. You're going to call them back, and if they're not in when you call, then you will have to leave your pager number again. They might call you back 20 minutes later, and by that time you could be in another meeting. You have some serious phone tag going on.

Instead of a pager number, leave your direct number. Let's say you, the customer, just called me and I'm in a meeting. As soon as the meeting is over I check the messages in my voice mail. I call you back immediately, but your office has to page you because you didn't answer your phone. When you call me back, instead of paging me, you're calling back on my direct line. It's more convenient for the customer, and the customer's convenience should be your priority.

Remember that you're not in business to service yourself, you're in business to service your customer. All these little things add up to better customer service. One of the biggest complaints from customers is that they can't reach their salesperson. Make it part of your sales presentation to say, "Mr. Johnson, your business is so important to me that I want you to have my direct line."

Giving out your direct line can eliminate the dead time that sales representatives would otherwise face between appointments. More frequent contact with customers and prospects means more opportunities for personal connections. Let your customers know that their calls are important by calling people back between appointments. I frequently say, "I just got your message and wanted to get right back to you on my way to my 2:00 appointment." It tells your customer that their call is so important to you that it warrants a fast response.

When you know you are going to be out of your office all day, be sure to give your secretary or assistant permission to give customers your evening number. Your customers aren't used to getting it, and years ago someone complimented me on doing that. If I am able to do so, I may return those calls before the next business day. It cuts down on the number of things I have to do the next morning, and it's another way to provide a high level of service to my customers. Let the customer be the one to say, "Oh, he doesn't need to call me back tonight. It can wait until tomorrow."

Returning Calls

Without a doubt, my No. 1 pet peeve would be people who don't bother to return calls, reply to email messages, or respond promptly to any other form of communication.

I will never understand why some people do not return calls immediately—not just in a timely manner, but IMMEDIATELY. We can all come up with examples of past experiences where we have called someone and left a message for them to call us back but they took several days to return the call or maybe didn't call us back at all.

One my favorites is when someone calls me back a couple of days later and says, "I'm sorry, but I've been so busy that I didn't have time to call you back." What that person is actually telling me could be any of the following things:

1. I have way too much business right now, and I don't need or want your business.

2. I have way too much business right now, and the company I work for gives me absolutely no support or help.

3. I am extremely lazy.

4. My spouse makes the majority of the income in my family, and I really don't need to work.

5. I don't think your business is that important to me.

6. I don't have a clue how to do business.

7. I don't like you.

I could go on and on, and I probably will until you get this message imbedded in your head and every fiber of your body.

Fact: When I was one of the busiest top producing real estate agents in the country and later when I was an owner of a very large real estate firm, guess what I did, not some of the time, but all of the time?

I RETURNED EVERYONE'S CALLS IMMEDIATELY!

That was my reputation; the word on the streets and from my customers, vendors, prospects—whoever—was "Van returns your calls right away. As busy as Van is, he always finds time to call you back in a timely manner."

I should add that I was not chatty on the phone, and I believe people respected the fact that I would "get to the meat" of the phone call and act accordingly. I would also let all my customers know upfront before they became customers that I was known for returning my calls very quickly, but to keep that reputation I would have to keep our conversations short and to the point.

When I first got involved in real estate sales, I would ask my customers what they liked and didn't like about the last time they used a Realtor. Basically, I wanted to find out their pet peeves upfront so I wouldn't make the same mistakes. The most common complaint, by a landslide, was "He took forever to return my calls." I couldn't believe that so many salespeople had slipped up in one of the easiest areas of business—communication. I knew how important it was to get back to customers right away, and I was careful to build a reputation in an area where others had failed.

All of this advice applies to email messages as well as phone calls. Reply immediately, even if you don't have the information they have requested. At the very least, send them a reply saying "Thank you for the email. I will get on this right away."

I currently live on a lake here in the city and last summer I noticed my sea wall was deteriorating and would need to be replaced. I made a total of three calls to contractors who did that kind of work. I called one and left a message on his voice mail telling him what I needed and asking him to call me back. No joke: I didn't get a phone call back that day, or the next day, or even the next week. Instead, I received a letter *three weeks later* that said, "I'm sorry, but I didn't get your message for some reason and I am writing to ask you to call me and set up an appointment for me to come out and look at your sea wall. Here is an address so you can check out one of the homes we did in your neighborhood." What? You have *got* to be kidding me! Nope, I never called him back and never will.

Salespeople and business people, listen up, please: if you don't believe that getting back to your customers *immediately* is a fundamental part of doing business, you are not thinking correctly.

My chosen career is real estate, and I know lots of people because of the field I am in. I am a networker and will tell everyone if I am pleased with the services I have received from someone I did business with. I spent over six figures putting in a pool years ago, and even though I am thrilled with the pool and its design and layout I can't refer the pool company. Can you guess why? Because the majority of the time when I had a question, which wasn't that often, I would leave the contractor a message and it took forever for him to get back to me. When people ask me about my pool I never mention the company's name because I am unable to speak highly of them as a result of their poor communication. I probably could have sent several dozen customers their way if they had returned my calls promptly.

If you work outside or out in the field all day, tell your customers or use your outgoing voice mail message to explain that you will return calls in the evening and to ask them to leave a number where they can be reached during the evening. Yes, it's that simple. What I am describing here is SERVICE. What our customers want is service and more service—not a difficult task if you want to stay in business.

It is truly a shame that I can give you many more examples of people who do *not* return calls in a timely manner than people who do. In my view, someone who returns my calls immediately is sending the following messages:

1. You are important to me.

2. Your business is important to me.

3. This is how I will do business with you if we end up doing business together.

4. I want your business.

5. Your time is valuable, and I respect that.

6. I understand that you called me today because you want to talk to me today.

I could go on and on about the fact that returning someone's calls quickly will show them how much you mean to them. As a business owner, I received many calls from local charities and fundraising organizations. Those were usually the calls that you really don't want to return right away, but I treated them the same way I would treat anyone else. The person who called you might end up being a customer someday or might know someone who could become a customer someday. Plus, bottom line—it's the right thing to do.

To recap: Return everyone's calls and emails in a timely manner and watch your business grow. Mine did, and I truly believe that my emphasis on returning calls was a huge contributor to my success.

University of
Nebraska at
Omaha

Intercollegiate Athletics
Omaha, Nebraska 68182
(402) 554-2305

November 16, 2000

Van Deeb
Deeb & Associates
11712 W Dodge Rd
Omaha, NE 68154

Dear Van,

Congratulations on being chosen to receive the Maverick Man of the Year Award at the
25th Annual UNO Athletic Hall of Fame Banquet.

Your contributions to our program of both time and money through the years have
impacted Maverick Athletics in so many ways. Our current successes are directly related
to your long term support.

We are proud to count you as a member of our family – UNO Athletics.

Sincerely,

Bob Danenhauer
Athletic Director

Cherri Mankenberg
Associate Athletic Director

University of Nebraska at Omaha   University of Nebraska Medical Center   University of Nebraska-Lincoln   University of Nebraska at Kearney

7 Quotations and Affirmations

"People often say that motivation doesn't last, but neither does bathing... that's why we recommend it daily." Zig Ziglar

Encountering the right motivational quote at the right time can make a huge difference in the way you handle situations that come up. Reading and connecting with just one inspirational, motivating quote or scripture daily may change the course of your day, your attitude, and your outlook in a specific area of your life.

On the following pages are some of my favorite quotes, and I hope many of them will soon be your favorites too.

I'll begin with an all-time favorite that I have used and abused many, times over the years: "The best way to predict the future is to create it." I don't know the name of the person who said it first, so I'll claim it as my own.

Staying Motivated

- "It is very important that you find something that you care about, that you have a deep passion for, because you are going to have to devote a lot of your life to it." George Lucas

- "If you think you can, or think you can't, you are probably right." Henry Ford

- "Work like you don't need the money. Love like you've never been hurt. Dance like no one is watching." Unknown

- "In the long run the pessimist may be proven right, but the optimist has a better time on the trip." Unknown

- "I always wanted to be somebody, but I guess I should have been more specific." Lily Tomlin

- "What isn't tried won't work." Claude McDonald

- "Stand for something or you will fall for anything." Unknown

- "Counting time isn't as important as making time count." Unknown

- "When a man is gloomy, everything seems to go wrong; When he is cheerful everything seems right." Proverbs 15:15

- " If you don't have an idea where you are going, you will never know if you've gotten there." Yogi Berra

- "Minds are like parachutes—they only function when open." Unknown

- "Yesterday is not ours to recover, but tomorrow is ours to win or lose." Lyndon B. Johnson

- "Be like a postage stamp—stick to one thing until you get there." Josh Billings

- "Action is the foundational key to all success." Pablo Picasso

- "Do not go where the path may lead; go instead where there is no path and leave a trail." Ralph Waldo Emerson

- Parable of the cautious man: "There was a very cautious man who never laughed or cried. He never risked, he never lost, he never won nor tried. And when he one day passed away, his insurance was denied, for since he never really lived, they claim he never died." Unknown

Habits and How They Affect You

- "Being miserable is a habit; being happy is a habit; and the choice is yours." Tom Hopkins

- "Mastering the fundamentals will make you a master and leader of your industry." Van C. Deeb

- "People who take action and fail are twice as likely to succeed as people who don't take any action at all." James O. Prochaska

- "People can be divided into three groups: those who make things happen, those who watch things happen, and those who wonder what happened." John W. Newbern

- "If you can dream it, you can do it." Walt Disney

- "The company you keep will determine the trouble you meet." Unknown

- "There is no method of success that will work unless you do." Unknown

- "The first step to wisdom is silence. The second is listening." Unknown

- "There are two kinds of people: the ones who need to be told and the ones who figure it out all by themselves." Tom Clancy

- "Wisdom is the reward you get for a lifetime of listening when you'd have preferred to talk." Doug Larson

- "If you're too busy to enjoy life, you're too busy." Jeff Davidson

- "Well done is better than well said." Unknown

- "Don't be afraid to go out on a limb. . . that's where the fruit is." Arthur F. Lenehan

- "One of the marks of superior people is that they are action-oriented. One of the marks of average people is they are talk-oriented." Brian Tracy

- "Life is like a ten-speed bicycle. Most of us have gears we never use." Charles M. Schulz

Doing Your Best

- "Many of life's failures are people who did not realize how close they were to success when they gave up." Thomas Edison

- "Perseverance is the hard work you do after you get tired of doing the hard work you already did." Newt Gingrich

- "One's philosophy is not best expressed in words; it is expressed in the choices one makes. In the long run, we shape our lives and we shape ourselves. The process never ends until we die. And the choices we make are ultimately our own responsibility." Eleanor Roosevelt

- "The quality of a person's life is in direct proportion to their commitment to excellence, regardless of their chosen field of endeavor." Vince Lombardi

- "You will find many things in your life that capture your eye, but very few will capture your heart. These are the ones to pursue. These are the ones worth holding on to." Van C. Deeb

- "I am a great believer in luck, and I find the harder I work, the more I have of it." Thomas Jefferson

- "Even if you are on the right track, you'll get run over if you just sit there." Will Rogers

- "Do what you can, with what you have, where you are." Theodore Roosevelt

- "If you're waiting for your ship to come in, make sure you sent one out." Unknown

- "No matter who you are, you don't have all the answers." Julie O'Brien

- "Many people are like a wheelbarrow—they go no further than they are pushed." Unknown

- "Half of being smart is knowing what you're dumb at." Unknown

- "Look at a day when you are supremely satisfied at the end. It's not a day when you lounge around doing nothing; it's when you've everything to do and you have done it." Margaret Thatcher

- "There is no better time than the present to be better than we were yesterday." Gary Kelley

- "Four short words sum up what has lifted most successful individuals above the crowd: *a little bit more*… They did all that was expected of them and a little bit more." A. Lou Vickery

Overcoming Adversity

- "Winners never blame anybody, it's only losers who try to blame other people for what went wrong, so never kid yourself that your failures and your weaknesses are somebody else's fault." Ron Barassi, Jr.

- "Follow the path of the unsafe, independent seeker. Expose your ideas to the danger of controversy. Speak your mind and fear less the label of 'crackpot' than the stigma of conformity." Thomas J. Watson, Jr.

- "Change should be exciting and enjoyable; it helps us grow into someone we have only dreamed about being. God gave us all the ability to be anything we want to be and accomplish anything we set our mind to." Van C. Deeb

- "Facing challenges and adversity will not always build our character, but it will certainly show us who we are by the way we deal with it." Van C. Deeb

- "I can't change the direction of the wind, but I can adjust my sails to always reach my destination." Jimmy Dean

- "Yesterday is a cancelled check; tomorrow is a promissory note. Today is the only cash you have, so spend it wisely." Kay Lyons

- "No one can make you feel inferior without your consent." Eleanor Roosevelt

- "A pessimist sees the difficulty in every opportunity; an optimist sees the opportunity in every difficulty." Unknown

- "Watch the little things... a small leak will sink a great ship." Benjamin Franklin

Putting People (Including Customers) First

- "You can have anything you want in life if you just help enough people get what they want." Zig Ziglar

- "Kindness is more important than wisdom, and the recognition of this is the beginning of wisdom." Theodore Isaac Rubin

- "When you are a leader in any business or organization, your people will work harder and will be happier if they know they are working with you and not for you." Van C. Deeb

- "Be sincere. People don't care how much you know until they know how much you care." Van C. Deeb

- "A leader's job is to look into the future and see the company or organization not as it is, but as it can become." Unknown

- The Road of Life: "I expect to pass through this world but once. Any good, therefore, that I can do or any kindness I can show any fellow creature, let me do it now... For I shall not pass this way again." Unknown

- "The true measure of a man is how he treats someone who can do him absolutely no good." Samuel Johnson

- "If your actions inspire others to dream more, learn more, do more and become more, you are a leader." John Quincy Adams

- "Cheerfulness is contagious, but don't wait to catch it from others. Be a carrier." Anonymous

- "Live so that your friends can defend you but never have to." Arnold H. Glasgow

- "A person who trusts no one can't be trusted." Jerome Blattner

- "Hardening of the heart ages people more quickly than hardening of the arteries." Unknown

- "Find the good and praise it." Alex Haley

- "Of all the things you wear, your expression is the most important." Unknown

- "The five most important words a leader can speak are: 'I am proud of you.' The four most important are: 'What is your opinion?' The three most important are: 'If you please.' The two most important are: 'Thank you.' And the most important single word of all is: 'You.'" Denis Waitley

- "Pretend that every single person you meet has a sign around their neck that says, 'Make me feel important.' Not only will you succeed in sales, you will succeed in life." Mary Kay Ash

- "They may forget what you said, but they will never forget how you made them feel." Carl W. Buechner

Attitude

- "Ambition is the path to success. Persistence is the vehicle you arrive in." Bill Bradley

- "Both poverty and riches are the offspring of thought." Napoleon Hill

- "Efforts and courage are not enough without purpose and direction." John F. Kennedy

- "Champions are not made in gyms; champions are made from something they have deep inside them: a desire, a dream, and a vision. They have to have the skill and the will. But the will must be stronger than the skill." Muhammad Ali

- "I had it in my heart. I believed in myself, and I had confidence. I knew how to do it, had natural talent and I pursued it." Muhammad Ali

- "Every achiever that I have ever met says, 'My life turned around when I began to believe in me.'" Dr. Robert Schuller

- "Excellence is the result of caring more than others think is wise, risking more than others think is safe, dreaming more than others think is practical, and expecting more than others think is possible." Unknown

- "You may have to fight a battle more than once to show you are the best and achieve victory. Never stop demonstrating what you believe in." Van C. Deeb

- "If you choose one phrase to repeat over and over again throughout your day, it should be 'There is nothing I can't do.'" Van C. Deeb

- "When a team of dedicated individuals makes a commitment to act as one, the sky is the limit." Unknown

- "Unless you try to do something that goes beyond what you have already achieved, you will never grow into your full potential." Van C. Deeb

- "The greatest discovery of any generation is that human beings can alter their lives by altering their attitudes." Albert Schweitzer

- "I have found that most people are about as happy as they make up their minds to be." Abraham Lincoln

- "A positive attitude may not solve all your problems, but it will annoy enough people to make it worth the effort." Herm Albright

- "Pessimism never won any battle." Dwight D. Eisenhower

- "Success is more a function of consistent common sense than it is of genius." An Wang

- "Find a job that you love and you will never have to work a day in your life." Jim Fox

- "Whatever the mind can conceive and believe, the mind can achieve." Napoleon Hill

- "It is not fair to ask of others what you are unwilling to do yourself." Eleanor Roosevelt

- "Age is something that doesn't matter unless you are cheese." Billie Burke (This quote is for Luke S., because he likes to say the word cheese…often!)

- "All we need to make us really happy is something to be enthusiastic about." Charles Kingsley

Dealing with Negativity and Discouragement
- "To escape criticism, do nothing, say nothing, be nothing." Elbert Hubbard

- "When you go in search of honey, you must expect to be stung by bees." Kenneth Kaunda

- "I am only one; but I am still one. I cannot do everything, but still I can do something. I will not refuse to do something I can do." Helen Keller

- "Not everything that is faced can be changed, but nothing can be changed until it is faced." James A. Baldwin

- "Only those who dare to fail greatly can ever achieve greatly." Robert F. Kennedy

- "You're never a loser until you quit trying." Mike Ditka

- "Whoever gossips to you will gossip of you." Spanish proverb

- "One of the secrets of life is to make stepping stones out of stumbling blocks." Jack Penn

- "The hardest thing to learn in life is which bridge to cross and which to burn." David Russell

- "If I had my life to live again, I'd make the same mistakes, only sooner." Tallulah Bankhead

- "Forgive your enemies, but never forget their names." John F. Kennedy

- "It is always helpful to learn from your mistakes, because then your mistakes seem worthwhile." Garry Marshall

- "I have always believed, and still believe, that whatever good or bad fortune may come our way we can always give it meaning and transform it into something of value." Hermann Hesse

- "You can tell more about a person by what he says about others than you can by what others say about him." Leo Aikman

- "Surround yourself with people most like the person you want to become. Stay away from anyone who can or will bring you down." Tom Hopkins

Handling and Overcoming Objections

- "Failure is not fatal, but failure to change might be." John Wooden

- "The idea of an overnight delivery service isn't feasible." A Yale business professor (in 1966) referring to a thesis submitted by Fred Smith, founder of FedEx

- "Depending on your view of the situation, a big challenge or problem can become one of your greatest opportunities." Van C. Deeb

- "The best way to convince a fool he is wrong is to let him have his way." Josh Billings

- "Obstacles are those frightful things you see when you take your eyes off your goals." Unknown

- "Experience is not what happens to you. It is what you do with what happens to you." Aldous Huxley

- "Success is how high you bounce when you hit bottom." General George S. Patton

- "Courage is being scared to death—but saddling up anyway." John Wayne (my favorite actor of all time)

- "Do what you feel in your heart to be right, for you'll be criticized anyway. You'll be damned if you do and damned if you don't." Eleanor Roosevelt

- "When one door closes another door opens; but we often look so long and so regretfully upon the closed door, that we do not see the ones which are open." Alexander Graham Bell

- "The few who dare are the envy of the many who only watch." Jim Rohn

- "A successful man is one who can build a firm foundation with the bricks that others throw at him." David Brinkley

- "Learn from the mistakes of others… you can never live long enough to make them all yourself." John Luther

- "Do just once what others say you can't… and you will never pay attention to their limitations again." James R. Cook

Business 101

- "Now, if you want to get rich, you have only to produce a product or service that will give people greater value than the price you charge for it. How rich you get will be determined by the number of people to whom you can sell the product or service." Earl Nightingale

- "If you aren't fired with enthusiasm, you will be fired—with enthusiasm." Vince Lombardi

- "Creativity is the power to connect the seemingly unconnected." William Plomer

- "There are no limits to our future if we don't put limits on our people." Jack Kemp

- "Watch, listen, and learn. You can't know it all yourself. . . anyone who thinks they do is destined for mediocrity." Donald J. Trump

- "You cannot help the poor by destroying the rich. You cannot strengthen the weak by weakening the strong. You cannot bring about prosperity by discouraging thrift. You cannot lift the wage earner by pulling the wage payer down. You cannot further the brotherhood of man by inciting class hatred. You cannot build character and courage by taking away men's initiative and independence.

You cannot help men permanently by doing for them what they could and should do for themselves." Abraham Lincoln

- "Formal education will make you a living; self-education will make you a fortune." Jim Rohn

- "Imagination is more important than knowledge." Albert Einstein

- "Your greatest strength is knowing your weakness." Jack Robson

- "Without promotion, something terrible happens: NOTHING!" P. T. Barnum

- "You have got to ask for your opportunities! Asking is, in my opinion, the world's most powerful and neglected secret to success and happiness." Percy Ross (I put this quote under Business 101 because I truly believe that if you are unwilling to ask for help and engage others in your quest, then you shouldn't be in business. I have been preaching to salespeople for years, "Ask for help, and watch your business grow.")

- "To succeed in sales, simply talk to lots of people every day. And here's what's exciting—there are lots of people." Jim Rohn

Goals, Goals, and More Goals
- "Not having a plan is like walking through a cave without a flashlight." Blake Fashing

- "Create a definite plan for carrying out your desire, and begin at once, whether you're ready or not, to put it into action." Napoleon Hill

- "Make no little plans; they have no magic to stir men's blood. Make big plans, aim high in hope and work." Daniel H. Burnham

- "I always have a plan for success. I have never made a plan for failure." Van C. Deeb

- "The tragedy of life doesn't lie in not reaching your goal. The tragedy lies in having no goal to reach." Benjamin E. Mays

- "Don't let the fear of the time it will take to accomplish something stand in the way of your doing it. The time will pass anyway; we might just as well put the passing time to the best possible use." Earl Nightingale

- "A dream is just a dream. A goal is a dream with a plan and a deadline." Harvey Mackay

- "Life is not so much a matter of 'finding' ourselves as it is a matter of making ourselves." Alan Loy McGinnis

- "The best opportunities in life are the ones we create. Goal setting provides for you the opportunity to create an extraordinary life." Gary Ryan Blair

Faith

- "Faith is taking the first step even when you don't see the staircase." Martin Luther King

- "Greatness is not in where we stand, but in what direction we are moving. We must sail sometimes with the wind or sometimes against it—but sail we must, and not drift, nor lie at anchor." Oliver Wendell Holmes

Dream Big

- "Set your sights high, the higher the better. Expect the most wonderful things to happen, not in the future but right now. Realize that nothing is too good. Allow absolutely nothing to hamper you or hold you up in any way." Eileen Caddy

- "Without leaps of imagination, or dreaming, we lose the excitement of possibilities. Dreaming, after all, is a form of planning." Gloria Steinem

- "You can dream, create, design and build the most wonderful idea in the world, but it requires people to make a dream a reality." Walt Disney

- "I dream for a living." Steven Spielberg

Failure Is Something We Can Learn From

- "One of the true failures in life is the failure to try something you believe in." Van C. Deeb

- "I don't know the key to success, but the key to failure is trying to please everybody." Bill Cosby

- "Failure is success if we learn from it." Malcolm S. Forbes

- "I have missed more than 9,000 shots in my career. I have lost almost 300 games. On 26 occasions I have been entrusted to take the game-winning shot... and missed. I have failed over and over again in my life... and that is why... I succeed." Michael Jordan

TESTIMONIALS

I feel like the most blessed man on earth to have been involved in so many people's professional lives. The following are testimonials from people I have had the privilege of working with, students who have heard my presentations, past customers, attendees in my sales/motivational seminars, Realtors, business owners, and community/business leaders. To all of these people I offer my heartfelt thanks. I am a better man because of the opportunity you gave me. By allowing me to help you, you helped me!

- "With Van's passion, humor and experience you can be assured of one thing: your audience is going to get fired-up, built-up, and fully charged-up. As an entrepreneur at the top of his game Van is in the unique position of being able to "talk the talk" because he has "walked the walk." Over the years he has been a great inspiration to me and my staff. Van is a speaker with charisma, humility and impact, and he's a difference maker in the lives of the people he touches."   George A.

- "It has been a pleasure to work for you. Your support and encouragement has made my transition into real estate easy and has given me the confidence to succeed."   Mike B.

- "Thank you so much for the continued support of Millard North High School athletics! Your efforts to help our youth are to be commended."   Dave P.

- "We are delighted you will be accepting the award for Omaha's Top 25 fastest growing companies. Congratulations on your outstanding growth, and we wish you continued success."   Tracey F.

- "I just want to wish you all the best. Because you're the best. Always there for all of us and so positive to all."   Mary D.

- "Thank you for running such a class act company. It is an honor and a pleasure to be associated with someone such as yourself. I know you are probably one of the most respected businessmen in the region."   Dustin T.

- "Congratulations on writing *Selling from the Heart* and thank you for sharing a copy with me. Your class has been one of the most enjoyable classes I've ever taken. Your enthusiasm and passion for your work are awesome. But the most refreshing part of the class was your delightful sense of humor. Thank you again for being a fantastic teacher."   Linda R.

- *"Magnificent* is clearly a word that describes you and your staff's attention in our relocation to Omaha." Henry B.

- "Wanted to send you a big THANK YOU for the great job you did for us. You certainly went above and beyond to get the job done. We really appreciate it."   Al and Bonnie R.

- "I wanted to thank you so much for chairing the Cystic Fibrosis Foundation's Bachelor/Bachelorette Auction. This event brought in much-needed funding to find a cure for cystic fibrosis. Thanks for your hard work and dedication."   Susan S.

- "Just a note to say we love your TV commercials; your daughter is a future movie star! Also thank you for all the things you do for Omaha. You are a huge asset to the community."   Jim G.

- "The students in our University of Nebraska sales class are still talking about your book and your presentation. Thank you for your time, energy and books you provided to the class. You never know when something like this will touch a life, and I think it is much more valuable than trying to learn it from a textbook. Please accept our deepest appreciation for your participation in our class this year. It has gone well, and your presentation was an important part of our success."   Roger L.

- "THANK YOU. YOU ARE THE REASON I WILL SELL REAL ESTATE FOR LIFE. From the minute I got licensed I was blessed that I was led through DEEB Realty's front doors. I never could have imagined that I would become a multi-million-dollar producer so soon in my real estate career, and I owe it all to you. My previous sales positions were just jobs with no passion and now I finally have a career for life that I love because of you! No one has ever motivated me with such high intensity and valuable tools that I can apply daily to make me more successful all around than you have. Thank you. You gave me some priceless smiles and laughs as I was going through a tough time trying to start a family while working at the office, so thank you just for being you! I just hope we will be fortunate enough for you to continue teaching your motivational courses to our agents to help everyone continue the high marks of success. You are the BEST of the BEST on motivating."   Tracy F.

- "Kudos to you, Van, for reaching a major goal. But more than that, for successfully building one of Omaha's best companies from scratch and making it thrive even in less-than-ideal market conditions. You have realized the American Dream and brought it home to many, many others. My best to you."   Todd A.

- "Best wishes for continued health and happiness. You are highly regarded and respected in the Omaha real estate and civic community."   Len H.

- "The City of Omaha and the metropolitan area continue to grow and prosper. Your efforts are a part of this success. On behalf of the mayor's office, I would like to thank you for your efforts and wish you good luck in the future."   B.H.

- "I would like to congratulate you on your recent Corporate Achievers Class award. There is no doubt that the value of your accomplishment is felt by all of us within Nebraska. Please accept my sincere appreciation for the fine job you are doing."   Larry K.

- "Your book is great! I have enjoyed the little free time I have reading your thoughts and am ready to put your ideas to use. I love your attitude and outlook on life. I can't wait to read your next book."   Jim G.

- "On behalf of the heartland children, thank you for the important part you have played in this year's Children's Miracle Network benefiting

Children's Hospital. The collective efforts of all involved will help us reach our year-end goal of $526,000 for the children. Thank you for helping Children's Hospital and the children we serve." Jane P.

- "On behalf of the City of Bellevue Department of Recreation, I would like to thank you for your generous support of the Youth Sports Program. With your donations the Department of Recreation continues to provide a quality program for young people of our community. Once again, thank you very much."   Jim S.

- "I am proud to have worked with such a giving person. I am grateful for all your guidance, support and leadership that you have shown me. I will miss hearing your laugh and being silly in your office. You made it fun to come to work. Thank you." Andrea S.

- "No Boss's Day card can truly convey how grateful I am to work for you. You are so generous with praise and showing your appreciation. I want you to know it isn't taken for granted. Coming to work is like being with friends and family, and I know you are largely responsible for creating such an atmosphere."   Dusti G.

- "I couldn't imagine working for any other broker. I think the world of you and your staff. I wish all the other Realtors got the chance to be a part of such a wonderful team and family. Thanks again for all that you do."   Marissa C.

- "It has been so great to be part of the company you started. Always on the cutting edge of something new AND DIFFERENT from the rest of the firms. I will always remember meeting you in the Southwest line at the airport a couple of years ago when I was going to real estate school trying to study for my licensing exam. You were so approachable and personable. Those are some of your gifts that are a big part of your success. All the best to you, Van! Thank you again."   Mindy H.

- "While you are on the circuit getting people fired up and excited about life, rest assured I am here to carry on your real estate legacy to all those that you have touched in such an admirable way. Know that you have been an inspiration to me since the day I walked into DEEB Realty and I have always admired your work ethic and genuine love of what you do. I have to also give you your due for all the wisdom you have shared over the years, and for reiterating, 'It's not rocket science. The most important thing is to treat people like they matter, and almost all the time, you'll be fine!' Thank you for those oh-so-true words." Sue H.

- "Just a short but very heartfelt note to say thank you for the wonderful company you have built through the years and the opportunity to work for you in real estate. I knew I'd found the right place from day one when I came to DEEB. It's been the best career opportunity and the greatest people here, and what you have built is a great tribute to you. I so appreciate all the motivation and education and the excellent support that I have always experienced here since I walked in the door almost five years ago. I will always be grateful to you for sharing your true passion for real estate with me and so many others. God bless you always." Michelle B.

- "I feel energized after our visit. You inspire me. You help me to think, live and be BIG. Thank you. You are a great man, and you are making an impact on other lives. I appreciate all you do." Jim G.

- "This note is long overdue. I really wanted to take the time to thank you personally and professionally for all that you have done for me and my family. You are a true motivator and a wonderful person to have in our life." Theresa O.

- "Just a short note to thank you for your valuable time. I really enjoyed our session yesterday; it was very inspiring."   Wayne

- "I just wanted to take the time to tell you how privileged I feel that I had an opportunity to listen and learn from you in the short time I have been at DEEB Realty. You are very inspirational and truly gifted in helping people go to the next level, whether it be in business or just in life. Not too many people can say that they have worked with such a phenomenal man."   Donna S.

- "Thank you for your generosity and support you have shown me over the past six years. You allowed me to develop at my own pace with no pressure and still continued to provide me with a wealth of information and knowledge you so graciously shared."   Kris S.

by john dechant

LEADING by Example

Omaha real estate magnate Van Deeb shows Deeb Realty is willing to lead the way in civic involvement.

The walls in Van Deeb's office are adorned head to toe with sports memorabilia. This expansive collection of artifacts isn't littered with signed photos from Heisman trophy winners or Cy Young award winners. Rather, Deeb's memorabilia contains photos and trophies from legion baseball teams and high school football camps. Framed and centered in the middle of this collection is a Deeb Mustangs baseball jersey with his surname printed on back: a symbol of thanks for nearly two decades of involvement with youth sports in Omaha.

As a former member of the University of Nebraska at Omaha football team, Deeb knows firsthand the benefits of participating in athletics. The qualities Deeb has used in becoming widely successful in the real estate industry were qualities ingrained into his psyche as a collegiate athlete by former Maverick football coach Sandy Buda. It's these same qualities – dedication, persistence and discipline – Deeb hopes to inspire in today's youth through his sponsorship of various sports programs throughout the city.

Tales of Deeb's civic involvement are well-known in the Omaha community. Since its inception in 1993, Deeb Realty has proudly supported organizations like the Children's Miracle Network, the American Cancer Society and the American Heart Association, but perhaps its greatest endeavors have been saved for youth sports. It all started in 1993 when the Deeb agency, then a fledgling startup organization of fewer than 10 real estate agents, was asked to sponsor a group of junior baseball teams in Bellevue. "We were a very small organization at the time and it was a very expensive endeavor to sponsor 250 kids back then," Deeb says. "But we did it then and we've continued to do it every year."

As Deeb's agency has flourished in the 15 years since it opened, his civic involvement has mirrored its growth. Deeb Realty has spread itself far and wide, sponsoring athletic programs throughout the city. Last year it footed the bill for a baseball camp at UNO and plans to do the same this year. It has also sponsored Millard North's athletic camps and summer legion baseball teams for years and has sponsored Central High School's summer baseball team for the last three years after rescuing it when it couldn't find a sponsor. "That's a great story," Deeb says of his association with Central. "I received a phone call from a parent three years ago asking if we'd consider sponsoring Central's summer baseball team, but unfortunately I had to tell them that we were already sponsoring so many other teams, I didn't think it was possible. The parent was very gracious and thanked me for my consideration, and then I got a phone call a few months later from the same parent, asking if we'd consider buying a banner for the field. I was told they still hadn't found a sponsor for the team and it was quite clear a lot of these kids simply couldn't afford to play baseball without a sponsor. As the oldest high school in the state with a who's who of successful graduates, I thought if we were able to afford it, we should really help them out. We're going on our third year now of sponsoring Central's summer baseball teams and it's been a great ride."

Deeb has even invited a few of the baseball players from Central's summer team to come in with their parents and sit down for informal motivational talks.

Next school year, Deeb Realty will be sponsoring intramural sports programs for elementary school children in the Omaha Public Schools. In all, the agency will be sponsoring over 2,500 children from 56 different public schools. Deeb's contributions will go directly towards outfitting these students with uniforms. The remaining portion of Deeb's sponsorship dollars assist in paying for facility fees and road trip costs that are a necessary part of funding sports programs.

Bob Danenhauer, Supervisor for Physical Education and Athletics for the Omaha Public School System, is a longtime Deeb confidant and a former teammate. The former UNO Athletic Director is quick to praise Deeb's contributions to the young athletes of Omaha. "Van loves supporting youth programs like legion baseball or intramurals because he grew up in that same environment and he continually wants to give back," he says. "We've never really seen another individual who's contributed so extensively."

Deeb's contributions are clearly extensive, but as a man who credits the discipline he received playing sports as one of the major factors in his professional success, encouraging young people to set goals and work for their dreams just comes with the territory. "If corporate America doesn't get involved with its young people, a lot of these programs are going to be forgotten," he says.

"And it's not just sports programs: band, debate, they all teach you about setting goals and working hard. Making a difference in the lives of young people is the most fulfilling feeling a person can get and seeing our competitors follow our lead is very gratifying."